About Father's House

A Revelation of the Heart of the Father for His People

Loren Covarrubias

Treasure House

An Imprint of
Destiny Image
P.O. Box 310
Shippensburg, PA 17257

"For where your treasure is
there will your heart be also." Matthew 6:21

ISBN 1-56043-815-0

For Worldwide Distribution
Printed in the U.S.A.

Treasure House books are available through these fine distributors outside the United States:

Christian Growth, Inc.
Jalan Kilang-Timor, Singapore 0315

Successful Christian Living
Capetown, Rep. of South Africa

Lifestream
Nottingham, England

Vision Resources
Ponsonby, Auckland, New Zealand

Rhema Ministries Trading
Randburg, South Africa

WA Buchanan Company
Geebung, Queensland, Australia

Salvation Book Centre
Petaling, Jaya, Malaysia

Word Alive
Niverville, Manitoba, Canada

Inside the U.S., call toll free to order:
1-800-722-6774

Acknowledgments

I am very grateful...

To Bonnie, my wife, co-laborer, and friend, for her untiring labor and constant love and support.

To Chris Legebow, for editing the manuscript and offering counsel.

To Ronda Ferguson, for preparing and processing the original manuscript.

This is
my Father's House,
and this is
His provision.

Contents

Introduction

Late at night on December 17, 1991, I was lying in bed unable to sleep. After a time, I decided to get out of bed to pray. Since 1991 was quickly coming to a close, I began to ask the Lord for direction for the new year. As I prayed, the presence of the Lord began to flood my soul. (I cherish such times when God comes so personally to renew His acquaintance with me.) I felt the coming year was to be a time of preparation for a new dimension in God.

As I sought the Lord, He told me to write a book about my experiences over the past 13 years of ministry. God instructed me to share the word that had been given to me and to explain how it had become a part of my being. God is looking for His word to become a manifested epistle, known and read of all men. The world needs a clear demonstration of the power of God. In His ultimate plan, God has chosen the Church to fulfill that purpose.

As for me, I felt God wanted to bring revelation to me, but first it was necessary to rehearse where I'd already been. By writing a book about my past ministry experiences, my foundation would be reaffirmed and I could continue building upon it. Matthew 13:12 says, "For whoever has, to him more will be given, and he will have abundance...." I looked for more because of what I had already seen. One great thing about the Kingdom of God is the more we receive, the more we can expect to receive.

My ministry began in 1978, the same year I completed Minister's Candidate School at Bethesda Missionary Temple in Detroit, Michigan. While there, I learned from my teacher, Patricia Beall Gruits, how to follow the way of the Spirit and the importance of a hearing ear. The apostle John said in his letters to the churches of Asia Minor, "He who has an ear, let him hear what the Spirit says to the churches" (i.e., Rev. 2:29).

We need ears that hear. The prophet Amos spoke of a famine in the land. This famine was not one of bread, but one of hearing God's word. We live in a time when the word goes forth in abundance. There is no shortage of listeners; rather, there is a shortage of hearers. My desire, from the beginning, has been to develop an ear to hear what the Lord is saying.

I believe a hearing ear is a gift from God. When Jesus came to the house of Israel, the Israelites did not hear the word He spoke. This was in direct fulfillment of Isaiah's prophecy, which Jesus quoted: "Hearing you will hear and shall not understand, and seeing you will see and not perceive" (Mt. 13:14). Jesus explained that Israel didn't hear because the people didn't have a heart for God. They honored God with their lips, but their hearts were far from Him. Jesus told His disciples that it was given to them to know the mysteries of the Kingdom of Heaven, but it was not given to the others (see Mt. 13:11).

Many Christians express their desire for the things of God, yet never make a strong commitment toward God. It may not be noticeable to man, but God knows because He sees the heart. God will only give a hearing ear to those whose hearts are right toward Him.

In Matthew 13:12, Jesus continued to say, "...but whoever does not have, even what he has will be taken away from him." When the word comes to us, it can lead us into a life of great spiritual prosperity—if we are willing and obedient. The more we prepare our hearts before God, the more His word will come to us. I have seen God's blessing multiply as I've prepared my heart and walked in obedience and God opened His word to me. It is a continual process of hearing, walking, and seeing the purposes of God unfold. It is exciting when God opens His word and lights the way for you.

I remember how God directed me to name the church *Mt. Zion Temple* and the outreach media *Call From the Mountain*. Isaiah 2:3 says that in the last days, "Many people shall come and say, 'Come, and let us go up to the mountain of the Lord, to the house of the God of Jacob; He will teach us His ways, and we shall walk in His paths.' For out of Zion shall go forth the law, and the word of the Lord from Jerusalem." This portion of Scripture has guided my ministry from the beginning.

Isaiah 2:2 reads, "...the mountain of the Lord's house shall be established on the top of the mountains, and shall be exalted above the hills; and all nations shall flow to it." Mt. Zion Temple will be a city on a hill that cannot be hid and a voice or call to the nations during the visitation that God is sending to the earth. This is the day when God is exalting His house so all nations will know where to turn in times of trouble. We, as Christians, must continually prepare our hearts before God so we can have ears to hear what the Spirit is speaking to the Church.

As I began writing this book, I intended its theme to be about the operation and function of a local church. However, the Lord showed me that it was to be about the Father's house. I immediately began to reflect back over my experiences of the past 13 years. Everything the Lord had spoken and all the chapters I had written came together. I realized that the Lord had been teaching me about His house all along. The time has now come when everything will be put in proper order because God wants to exalt His house. The Church must make herself ready in order that she, in unison with the Spirit, can beckon the lost to come. "And the Spirit and the bride say, 'Come!' And let him who hears say,

'Come!' And let him who thirsts come. Whoever desires, let him take the water of life freely" (Rev. 22:17).

The underlying premise of this book is that the Lord is building His house line upon line, precept upon precept. The lost will never run to a house built by man.

In the mid-1980s, the Lord gave me a vision of a great city falling into ruins. It was so great that the debris rose up to the sky. The Lord told me there would be many major ministries falling in the days ahead. Then, in the vision another city arose from the midst of the rubble and debris. The Lord said it was an unshakable kingdom, the Kingdom of God.

It wasn't long before scandalous reports of many well-known ministries began hitting the headlines. These stories represented things happening all over the world. Man's work crumbles and falls, but a house built by the Father will be exalted—even the gates of hell shall not prevail against it. Out of the midst of human failure, the Kingdom of God will arise in glory.

I am honored to write about my Father's house because I've always loved the house of the Lord. I remember giving my life to God when I was only four years old; I had answered an altar call at Vacation Bible School. Now, my experiences in church have not always been good, but my relationship with the Father has sustained me and I want so much for His house to be everything He desires.

Today the organized church does not have a very good reputation. Statistics show that 75 percent of the population in the United States believes in Jesus Christ and the Bible and 98 percent believe in God; yet, only 40 percent actually attend church. In many areas this percentage is considerably lower. When the Church becomes all that the Father intends, the nations of the earth will indeed say, "Come, and let us go up to the mountain of the Lord, to the house of the God of Jacob."

Obviously, the Father's house should be a direct reflection of Himself. I have served God all of my life, not because of the church, but in spite of it. It is unfortunate that many people have been offended and wounded by organized religion. Change must come because God's house, His Church on the earth, is not for convenience; it is a necessary part of His plan.

The Father wants His house to be a witness in the earth. The local church, the place of His corporate presence, is a testimony and a witness of His covenant with man. When we corporately submit to His purpose, we invoke the blessing of God in our midst.

On the Isle of Patmos, John received the revelation of Jesus Christ. To understand this revelation, we must see the Church as His Body, the fullness of Him who is all in all (see Eph. 1:23). At the end of the book, John saw the tabernacle of God descending out of Heaven, coming down to men. This glorious tabernacle is the beauty of the Church. Isaiah prophesied that the Lord will glorify the house of His glory (see Is. 60:7). When we offer God an acceptable abiding place and seek to make His house glorious, He will place His *shekinah* or manifest glory upon it. The house will then truly become a tabernacle that witnesses to the whole earth.

As you read *About Father's House*, you will see that God laid one revelation upon another in building Mt. Zion Temple. Each stone or principle has been laid first with a revelation of God's purpose, and then with my obedience or submission to that word. As we learn one principle, God adds another.

In John 12, Jesus, when predicting His own death, spent a great deal of time preparing the disciples for the changes that would occur. He said, "...But for this purpose I came to this hour. Father, glorify Your name" (Jn. 12:27-28). When Jesus said this, a voice came from Heaven saying, "I have both glorified it and will glorify it again" (Jn. 12:28). As John 1:14 reads, "...we beheld His glory, the glory as of the only begotten of the Father, full of grace and truth." This glory would now be released to its fullest potential. The Father had glorified His name through Jesus Christ and would now glorify the house of His glory through the Church.

Jesus declared, "This voice did not come because of Me, but for your sake. Now is the judgment of this world; now the ruler of this world will be cast out. And I, if I am lifted up from the earth, will draw all peoples to Myself" (Jn. 12:30-32). Note also that Jesus said, "If anyone serves Me, let him follow Me; and where I am, there My servant will be also. If anyone serves Me, him My Father will honor" (Jn. 12:26). Jesus said if we serve Him, we will be where He is. He was not talking merely about a location, but rather an experience.

In order to walk in the footsteps of Jesus, we must first become a testimony of the Father and then offer our lives for His purpose. When we surrender everything to God, we move into another dimension of His glory. First the glory was *in* Jesus, but now it will be manifested *through* Him. As we submit our lives to God, His glory is revealed in us. When we totally die to our selfish purposes, then His purpose, the reason we were born, will be accomplished.

Although Jesus had accomplished much in His life to the glory of the Father, the real moment of decision came at the garden of Gethsemane. There, in intense turmoil, Jesus fully submitted Himself to the Father's will. At that moment of total surrender, His struggle ended. Satan could not dissuade Him. When Jesus completely submitted Himself, the power of the enemy was judged by His righteous witness. When our obedience is complete, He will avenge all disobedience.

It is at the point of our complete surrender that the place of God's presence becomes the place of His testimony. In the Old Testament, God's presence dwelt on an ark; it was known as the ark of His testimony, the ark of witness, or the ark of the covenant. It was not just a witness of God's presence in the midst of His people; it was also a visible testimony of God and His covenant.

Today, the Father is looking for the place of His presence to become a place of testimony or a witness of His covenant with man. As we submit to the Father, our lives bear testimony to His faithfulness and to His covenant with man. He, in return, places His blessing upon our lives and glorifies the house of His glory.

When we have submitted ourselves to the purposes of God, we will see the glory of God upon us in a new dimension. As you read the principles contained in this book, be aware of their twofold application. Our Father's house is first the Church, a collective effort of a many-membered body. But, as you read about the Father's house being a house of planting, remember it also applies to you individually. Each principle should be studied in relationship to its corporate and its personal application.

At the beginning of my ministry, I set out to build something for God, only to discover that He was more concerned about building something in me. When our house is complete, His house will be complete. Prepare your heart before the Lord and ask Him to show you a glimpse of His house. It is His desire that we all partake of this marvelous work that He has purposed for our day, the exaltation of His house. My prayer is, "Father, come now and glorify the house of Your glory!"

Chapter 1

A House of Planting

In the spring of 1978, I was in prayer about a small Bible study group taught by my mother. She had a great desire to teach and with some urging from her friends, started a class in our home using the text, Understanding God, written by Patricia Beall Gruits. We had, through the teaching of my mother, been given a strong Christian foundation based upon Hebrews 6:1-3: "...let us go on to perfection...." I felt responsible for these people and wanted to make sure they continued to spiritual maturity, but I did not feel any of the area churches could adequately nurture them. Thus, I needed definite direction from God for the future of this small Bible study group. I also needed direction for my own life, as I was just completing Minister's Candidate School (MCS), which was taught by Patricia Beall Gruits.

I had been asked to speak at my Minister's Candidate School graduation ceremony and the word God had spoken to me was "guard the seed." This not only became my topic for graduation, it also set the course and direction for my ministry. I used First Peter 1:22-23 as the text for my message:

Since you have purified your souls in obeying the truth through the Spirit in sincere love of the brethren, love one another fervently with a pure heart, having been born again, not of corruptible seed but incorruptible, through the word of God which lives and abides forever (1 Peter 1:22-23).

God wanted me to understand the importance of guarding the incorruptible seed that He had placed in the lives of the people in the Bible study group and to realize the awesome potential in each one.

The Father is waiting for the precious fruit of the earth. We need to satisfy His desire to see His people bring forth fruit. This is only possible if the seed is not lost. The beginning of my divine commission was to guard the seed that the Father had planted in the hearts of the people placed under my ministry. Their growing process was like the one I remembered observing in school. Each pupil was instructed to keep a seed moist under a clear glass. After the seeds sprouted, we planted them in soil, where they grew into productive plants.

I shared this word about guarding the seed with my MCS graduating class. I told them how we had experienced great things in God, but that we needed to realize we were just immature sprouts. We had experienced spiritual watering, but this was only the beginning of the growing process. To continue growing toward full maturity or fruitfulness, we had to be planted in good ground. I also shared this word with the people in our small Bible study group. The life that had sprung forth was exciting to watch, but the Father wanted more. He was looking for fruitfulness.

I continued seeking for direction. I needed assurance that God's purpose for me was to start a church. One day, as I was praying, the Spirit of the Lord came strongly upon me and I began to prophesy, "I will make you a vessel of the new wine and I will give you a people that out of their midst shall flow the wine of the Lord...multiplication and increase...multiplication and increase." At that point, I knew I was to start a church.

Being confident that the mantle of ministry was firmly upon me, I began to prepare myself for the work ahead by inquiring of the Lord what this word meant. He amplified its meaning to me as well as set me on a journey toward its fulfillment. Proverbs 29:18a says, "Where there is no vision, the people perish" (KJV) and I knew that with this vision I had definite direction.

New Wine

As I studied, the Lord showed me that *new wine* is the product of the fruit of His vine, or the vine of the Church, each member of the Body of Christ being a branch. It is important for the Church to maintain an environment where fruit can be brought to maturity.

As the fruit of the Spirit develops in us, we mature and ultimately reach a level where we can produce wine. Fruitful people, under pressure, will draw from the power of God and begin to pour forth new wine. However, unfruitful people under pressure have nothing to pour forth and so will not be preserved. When Jesus faced the pressure of His life, He poured out life and healing to all nations. This is exactly what the Father has purposed for each of us.

We must remember that in order to preserve new wine, it must be stored in new wineskins. Jesus said, "And no one puts new wine into old wineskins; or else the new wine bursts the wineskins, the wine is spilled, and the wineskins are ruined..." (Mk. 2:22). If we want to preserve the new wine, we must have the proper containers. Thus, the responsibility of the Church is twofold. First, we must provide and maintain a proper environment for producing fruit. Second, we must keep our wineskins flexible, so they will be able to contain the new wine that is poured out by God.

Many churches have sought for and experienced great moves of God, but their wineskins (or structures) have not been flexible enough to handle God's pouring forth. Many churches have not allowed God the opportunity to move and so have burst. They preferred their man-made structures to moving with God. Many times structures are damaged or even destroyed because of their failure to change. That is why many people associate a move of God with their having many problems. We must be careful to ensure that full preparation has been made for change because God will judge us on how we handle the move of God in our midst. I believe the local church is intended to be a flexible structure, one that will fully adapt to and accommodate the move of God.

Grounding the Seed

Let me again emphasize the importance of guarding the seed. In the parable of the sower in Matthew 13, Jesus explained how seed can be robbed of its purpose. He spoke about seed falling by the wayside where it was eaten by birds; the seed falling on stony ground where it would spring forth, yet die because it could not take root; the seed falling among thorns where it was choked; and the seed falling on good ground where it yielded much fruit.

The fate of the seed is contingent upon the condition of the ground (human hearts) where it is planted. He who receives seed by the wayside represents anyone who hears or receives the Word but does not understand it. The word *understand* in this passage means to put together or comprehend, which implies more than just an awareness. It is an intentional or planned process of planting.

The *wayside* represents an unintentional planting of seed; perhaps it has seed that was scattered or dropped along the way. In the natural realm, the greatest way to ensure the continuation of a species is the scattering of seed. However, from a Kingdom standpoint, this is not true. The incorruptible seed must be planted in a well-tended garden—not a *wayside* place or in the wild.

God desires a mature plant that has been carefully tended and developed by the Husbandman, not a stunted plant that barely exists. Jesus said, "I am the true vine and My Father is the vinedresser. ...you are the branches..." (Jn. 15:1,5). In order for seed to mature and bring forth desired fruit, it must be under the care of the Master Husbandman.

As guardians of the seed, we need to have a full understanding of God's plan for it. When we understand God's purpose for our lives, then the seed has truly been planted; this ultimately provides the greatest protection from the birds of the air that seek to devour it.

When I was a child, I remember being tempted by our neighbor's strawberry patch. Mr. Hamilton's carefully tended plants always produced the largest, sweetest strawberries. In our yard, right next to his patch, grew wild strawberry plants that produced small, sour berries. There was a big difference in the size and taste of the berries because of the place of planting and the care of the seed. In Isaiah 5:1-2, the prophet declares,

> *Now let me sing to my Well-beloved a song of my Beloved regarding His vineyard...on a very fruitful hill. He dug it up and cleared out its stones, and planted it with the choicest vine. He built a tower in its midst, and also made a winepress in it; so He expected it to bring forth good grapes, but it brought forth wild grapes* (Isaiah 5:1-2).

The Scriptures say that God will destroy the vineyard of wild grapes. God is not looking for a wild variety, but one carefully tended and developed by the Husbandman.

He who receives seed on stony places hears and immediately receives the Word, yet the seed cannot take root and it endures only for a while. When the sun appears, it immediately withers away. In the stony place (or unplowed ground), it is impossible for the seed to take root and without a root system, a plant cannot receive the vital nutrients needed for survival. God has created each plant to adapt to the seasons by relying on heavenly and earthly sources of life.

Many people come to church and readily receive the Word, but they never allow the Word to take root in their lives. The local church should be a place where the ground of people's hearts can be regularly cultivated and kept soft and workable, so the seed can take root and receive the right nutrients to reach full maturity.

A good farmer is aware that he must deal with and prepare for the changes and unpredictability of the seasons. He knows that without patience, persistence, and hard work, he will not have lasting results. God, the Husbandman of the whole earth, has much patience. Because of His character, we can rely upon Him to produce the new wine in our lives. When Mt. Zion Temple began, I set out hoping to change everyone. I didn't realize that God was using them to change me. God had said to me, "I will make *you* a vessel of the new wine...." We may not always see the result of our labor, but we will see the result of God's faithfulness. Isaiah 54:1-2 says,

> *"Sing, O barren, you who have not borne!...For more are the children of the desolate than the children of the married woman," says the Lord. "Enlarge the place of your tent, and let them stretch out the curtains of your habitations; do not spare; lengthen your cords, and strengthen your stakes"* (Isaish 54:1-2).

We cannot grow and mature in God unless we are willing to change. The fallow ground of our lives must be broken up so the life of God can flourish. We must be pliable to house the wine of God.

After we realize our need to be planted with purpose and are open to change, we must set proper priorities. The seed sprouting among thorns represents anyone hearing the Word whose preoccupation with the cares of the world chokes the Word. We must be planted in soil that is kept free of weeds. If the weeds are not removed, they will live at the expense of the seed.

As a young boy, I remember wanting to be a farmer. Mr. Hamilton's garden yielded many vegetables year after year, so I decided to plant a garden of my own. I could hardly wait to pick my own vegetables, but I soon found out that being a farmer wasn't at all what I'd thought. Weeds took over my garden; the plants became unhealthy and did not bear much. The radish plants grew almost two feet tall, but when I pulled them out of the ground, there were no radishes—just roots. They had gone to seed because I had not thinned them out early in the growing season. I found out that I not only had to weed my garden, but also choose from among the good seed; I had to choose which plants were to grow all the way to fruitfulness.

The things we do for God need to be prioritized. Otherwise we may risk the chance of not producing fruit. I discovered that I had never wanted to be a farmer; I really wanted to be a harvester. To see a harvest, though, we must first become consistent and responsible farmers. The whole Kingdom of God is built on the premise of the harvest. If we set priorities based on the Word of God, we will begin to weed out those things that would inevitably choke out our life.

Finally, in the parable of the sower, the seed planted in good ground is the only seed that matures to fruitfulness. Just as my garden could not produce without proper attention, so is the Body of Christ. We must have the help of the Husbandman. He patiently cares for us until we produce fruit. This does not mean that He is lazy or has a passive commitment to the harvest; instead He has an interactive long-term commitment.

Maturing the Seed

Jesus said that the Father will prune us and work with us until we bear much fruit. We need to understand the difference between what man is supposed to do and what only God Himself can do. An overemphasis in either direction will lead to the loss of the full blessing of God. Let us study God's Word realizing that we are co-laborers together with Him.

Just as the Husbandman has much patience for the earth to bring forth fruit, so must those who labor with Him. If we are yoked together with God, His fruit will be produced in us. Because the growing and maturing process takes considerable time, we must learn to be longsuffering and patient—two significant characteristics of the fruits of the Spirit. There probably is no other vocation that relies more on the character of the worker than on the type of work. A farmer not only commits to the relentless work involved, but he also commits to a life style. He must learn to flow with the seasons and not be easily discouraged. No matter how unpredictable the season, he remains focussed on his long-range plan.

You may recall times when your plans were ruined because of inclement weather and you were especially disappointed because you had no control over it. It must be devastating for a farmer to lose his very sustenance because of poor or severe weather conditions. To survive, a farmer must plan for those times. He knows that as long as he has seed, there is potential for life. Hebrews 6:12 says, "...do not become sluggish [lazy], but imitate those who through faith and patience inherit the promises."

After spring planting, a farmer only hopes for a harvest—he has no guarantee. The only thing he can do is wait. He can neither rush the season nor speed up the growing process. He knows that the keys to success are always the same: work, faith, and patience. The purpose of God for the Church always evolves from these same three keys.

10

In Psalm 92:12, David said, "The righteous shall flourish like a palm tree, he shall grow like a cedar in Lebanon." The palm grows very quickly and flourishes where other trees will not. When we first begin serving God, it is not unusual to see the hand of God working for us in a quick and exciting way.

On the other hand, the cedar grows very slowly, yet its life span far exceeds that of the palm. The cedar is recognized by its beauty, height, and strength. Lebanon was known for its magnificent forests of cedar that once graced its mountains. Like a cedar, we must grow sure and strong. It may take a lifetime for us to become what God has purposed.

Too often the need for immediate results lends itself to actions that do not bring long-term blessing. Our short-term accomplishments are important, but only that which is produced and matured in us over time will remain. Psalm 92:13-15 continues, "Those who are planted in the house of the Lord shall flourish in the courts of our God. They shall still bear fruit in old age; they shall be fresh and flourishing, to declare that the Lord is upright; He is my rock, and there is no unrighteousness in Him."

When I started Mt. Zion Temple, my expectations were high. As I mentioned, I did not realize the importance of the word God had spoken to me, "I will make *you*." When God speaks a word about His people, our first response is to try to change the people. The Father, in His wisdom, knows that the word must first work in the one who receives it.

11

When Joseph received a word from God, the Lord tried him until that word came to pass. Joseph was destined to be a man of authority, but the 17-year-old boy who received the dream, although willing, was not mature enough. God began a process that matured and transformed Joseph through his many experiences. He became a fruitful bough whose branches ran over the wall.

In each phase of his life, Joseph remained faithful to God and so prospered. He never lost his vision. When the time came for the fulfillment of the Father's purpose, it simply continued the pattern of fruitfulness that had been established throughout his life. Even the difficult times only enhanced the blessing that Joseph would walk in during his latter days. If we understand the power in the seed and the principle of being planted in God's Word, we can learn to enjoy the maturing process of our lives and trust that a special blessing is reserved for our latter days. This is the Father's plan for all of us.

Thus the Father had instructed me to carefully tend the seed in the lives of those that had been planted in our midst. I knew that I had to guard the seed. As I obeyed God's instruction, He tended and cultivated the seed in me. I knew my responsibility was to stay planted. Psalm 1:3 says that the righteous "shall be like a tree planted by the rivers of water, that brings forth its fruit in its season, whose leaf also shall not wither; and whatever he does shall prosper."

A person who is planted will have winter seasons, but he will also have fruit-bearing seasons. A tree can naturally survive any season as long as it remains planted. Our adherence to the Word must remain our constant focus. We can receive power and strength by meditating upon it. The dream or vision of God is then ever before us.

I have found that if I remain focused on the promise and planted in the whole counsel of His Word, I can bear fruit even during adverse times. The dream God has for me keeps me planted and I know that in God's time, His word to me will come to pass. Joshua received instruction not to let the book of the law depart from his mouth, but to meditate in it day and night so he would observe to do all that was written. Then he would be prosperous and successful. (See Joshua 1:8.) The Father's house is first and foremost a house of planting.

A Challenging Vision

On Wednesday night, March 15, 1989, I was praying in a group with several others at the church. As I began to pray in tongues, I saw in the spirit a woman preparing a meal. She was stirring something in a bowl. This picture did not leave my mind for some time. Finally, I sensed a change in the direction of my prayer and I saw another woman kneeling with a pen in her hand and paper on her lap. In my spirit, I heard *"escribe la vista, escribe la vista, escribe la vista."* I repeated these words aloud.

Lolly Dye, who was also there in prayer, told me that she had seen a vision at the same time that I did. She had seen inside a vast, breathtaking mansion that appeared to extend for miles. She said that the verse,

"In My Father's house are many mansions..." (Jn. 14:2), came to mind and it appeared to be just one of the many dwelling places of the Holy Spirit. As she looked around inside the mansion, there were many servants who appeared to be the Body of Christ, members of the congregation of Mt. Zion Temple. Working in one mind, one accord, and one spirit, the servants were preparing for the feast that the King had ordered. There was a feeling of excitement and joy in the air. Their thoughts were so harmonious that verbal communication was unnecessary. Each servant was busy carrying out their orders. The silverware, china, candlesticks, and table linen were of the finest quality. Everything necessary for preparation was supplied from a never-ending source.

The servants each had their own intricate tasks and carefully performed them. Everyone knew what to do. Lolly noticed my mother carrying baskets of luscious fruit to be placed on the tables. She immediately thought of my mother's teachings regarding the fruit of the Spirit—love, joy, peace, longsuffering, kindness, goodness, faithfulness, gentleness, and self-control.

Lolly explained that while everyone was working, she noticed an enormous set of doors that extended up to the ceiling. As she looked outside through the doors, she saw multitudes of people coming toward the mansion. The servants were ready to receive all of them; they were never concerned about meeting their needs. She said at that moment, she tried to shake off what was happening. She thought perhaps she had been daydreaming. But then she focused on one man in particular walking with crutches. She said that I immediately began speaking in tongues in Spanish *"vienen con muletas,"* describing what she was seeing in the Spirit. (Lolly is bilingual and was able to interpret.) I had said that they would come on crutches.

She then focused upon a sorrowful woman who appeared to have a broken heart. I began speaking *"vienen quebrados,"* which means they come broken.

She again focused upon another man who appeared to be wounded and bleeding. I began speaking *"vienen heridos,"* which means they come wounded.

Lolly said when she opened her eyes and looked over at me praying, I was saying *"escribe la vista, escribe la vista, escribe la vista,"* which means "write the vision." God had tied the two visions together as a confirmation to us for Mt. Zion Temple. It was a miraculous demonstration of the gift of tongues. Lolly knew I did not speak Spanish, yet she heard me speak it. It was only by the inspiration of God that I was able to speak and confirm the vision of fruitfulness that God had given to us in the beginning.

This challenge to minister to those who have failed or who have been wounded, however, requires a great deal. We must make a commitment for life. We shouldn't look so much for the miraculous, but watch for the long-term development of God's Word—from the planting of the seed through to fruitfulness and harvest. I understand that the Father's house is a house of planting and that if I commit myself to the growing and maturing process of God, I will one day produce fruit beneficial to others.

Chapter 2

A Spiritual House

After God prompted me to start a church with the group meeting in our home, I immediately began looking for a building to worship in, having in mind an old house or perhaps a traditional storefront that could be renovated. A friend in real estate told me about a church building close by. Several people from our group drove over to look at the building. We were overwhelmed because it was more than what we ever expected to find. However, the asking price was $220,000, far beyond what we could afford. There were less than 20 adults in our small group; only five were employed. I thanked the realtor and informed him that it wasn't exactly what we were looking for.

That night, while in prayer about the purchase of a church building, the Lord spoke a strong word to me.

"If you will go the way of the Spirit, you will possess things others have not possessed!" Because of my own thinking, I had limited my expectation in God. This word, though, set me in the right direction. In my heart, I knew it was God's desire that we obtain this particular building. So He would certainly make a way for us to do it. However, we would have to walk the way of the Spirit, step out in faith, and not waver at the promises of God. The way of the Spirit is not a decision to do what we think we should do for God, but to find out what His will or purpose for us is.

This word set the pace for the overall ministry of Mt. Zion Temple and is the key to fulfilling God's desire and purpose for the church. When I discussed the purchase some more with the realtor, he said the minimum we could offer was $180,000, which would require a $40,000 down payment. I went ahead, in faith, and made an offer to purchase the church—having only a few thousand dollars.

Our group began raising money (bake sales, garage sales, etc.) and had accumulated almost $15,000 when we received word that the seller would accept $190,000 if we could come up with a $45,000 down payment. We agreed to those terms even though we didn't have $40,000. What difference would another $5,000 make?

We were walking by faith, but our commitment to this walk in the Spirit was being challenged because the finances simply were not there. We began seeking the Lord further. One day, the Lord gave me a song, *Give Me Faith, Lord, to Believe in Miracles.* As I sang it throughout the day, the Lord began to fill me with faith. The Word declares, "So then faith comes by hearing, and hearing by the word of God" (Rom. 10:17). When I shared this simple song and message with the group, we were all edified. God sovereignly began putting the finances in our hands. However, on the day of closing, we were still $10,000 short. I remember going to work that day, my faith not wavering, for God's word had put me in the dimension of the Spirit.

In the middle of the day, my mother came by to tell me that the husband of a lady in our group had intended to invest some money in a business deal that had apparently fallen through. He asked his wife if the church could use $10,000. God had made a way for us! At the end of that day, we had $45,000 in hand and the purchase was completed. God was faithful to His word.

From this experience, God not only taught me the way of possessing His promises, but He also established an order and structure for our church; we must rely on the Spirit and hear God's word. The rallying point for any move of God must be the anointed word or vision given by God. No man-made structure can sustain a move of God on its own. In Matthew 16, Jesus asked His disciples this very important question: "Who do men say that I, the Son of Man, am?" (Mt. 16:13) The disciples replied, " 'Some say John the Baptist, some Elijah, and others Jeremiah or one of the prophets.' He said to them, 'But who do you say that I am?' Simon Peter then answered and said, 'You are the Christ, the Son of the living God' " (Mt. 16:14-16). Peter had revelation knowledge of Jesus. Jesus then answered and said to him, "Blessed are you, Simon Bar-Jonah, for flesh and blood has not revealed this to you, but My Father who is in heaven. And I also say to you that you are Peter, and on this rock I will build My church, and the gates of Hades shall not prevail against it" (Mt. 16:17-18). Jesus was not referring to Peter, the man, when He spoke of the rock, but to the revelation knowledge that Peter spoke.

A Living Word

When God gives a visionary word, its purpose will always be to give us direction as a people and to provide us an opportunity to see Him more clearly. Peter wrote in Second Peter 1:4, "By which have been given to us exceedingly great and precious promises, that through these you may be partakers of the divine nature...." We can only experience a living Christ from a living word.

A revealed word becomes the foundation of the Church and is the only thing God will build upon. Because God is a God of order, structures will follow. However, without a living word as the foundation, the structure will become an organization, not a living organism. First Corinthians 3:11 says, "For no other foundation can anyone lay than that which is laid, which is Jesus Christ."

Church history records that all true moves of God were birthed from someone's firsthand encounter with God. The early Church was birthed when the disciples began preaching about the resurrection of Christ that they had witnessed. As Paul received great revelation

20

on the road to Damascus, multitudes rallied around his witness and the Gentile church was founded.

The leaders of great movements in the Church always experienced an encounter with God that motivated them to minister. For example, Augustine was a great foundational leader of the Catholic faith; Martin Luther and John Calvin were the chief founders of Reformation theology; George Whitefield was responsible for the Great Awakening in England; John Wesley preached salvation and renewal, transforming the spiritual and moral theology of England; Charles Wesley (the brother of John) produced over 7,000 sacred songs and poems, many of which are still sung today; and on and on throughout Church history. These men, like Peter and Paul, personally received a revelation word from God that reached and transformed nations.

All true moves of God begin in the Spirit, but the problem is, many do not continue in the Spirit. Paul asked the Galatians, "Are you so foolish? Having begun in the Spirit, are you now being made perfect by the flesh?" (Gal. 3:3) God has instructed us not only to start in the Spirit, but also to continue walking in the Spirit! This can be difficult because, as the Bible says, "the carnal mind is enmity against God; for it is not subject to the law of God, nor indeed can be" (Rom. 8:7).

We in the Protestant Movement balk at the Catholic interpretation of Matthew 16 that says Jesus built His Church not on the revelation of the Word, but upon Peter himself and that the apostolic succession continues through the Pope, the only true authority. We've always been taught that the Catholic church built its foundation on man rather than on God; yet we Protestants have followed a similar pattern. Lutherans, Wesleyans, Calvinists, etc., are denominations or institutions built upon men. We must realize that God wants to build a foundation on the revelation first given to a person, and then to continue building with new revelation.

The Anointing vs. the System

There is direction given in the Scriptures to help us avoid building an institution upon or to the honor of men; however, we tend to misinterpret it. In writing to the Corinthian church, Paul spoke about their immaturity. One would say, "I am of Apollos," and another would say, "I am of Cephas" (see 1 Cor. 1–3). We have generally interpreted these passages to mean that we are not to be followers of men like the Corinthian church was. However, we should be followers of men. Paul sums it up by saying in First Corinthians 4:15-16, "For though you might have ten thousand instructors in Christ, yet you do not have many fathers; for in Christ Jesus I have begotten you through the gospel. Therefore I urge you, imitate me." He continues saying in chapter 11, "Imitate me, just as I also imitate Christ" (1 Cor. 11:1). The key is to follow the spiritual life of the man of God.

Most people seeking and hungering after the things of God will recognize and respond to the anointing that is upon someone. Problems arise when it is time for them to make a decision to follow that anointing. They fear that they will be labeled *followers of men*, and forget that it was the anointing that motivated them to submit in the first place.

Often religious systems stray from the truth. They don't understand God's divine order of walking the way of the Spirit. This pattern is particularly evident in the local church setting. God raises up an anointed person to lead the flock of God and many people gather to the sound of the anointed voice. Then, during a time of transition when the Lord is raising up a new voice, many people stay married to the system and will not leave to follow the move of God. The people most prominent in the former move are the ones who tend to fight the hardest. They protect the system and choose their positions in the church over the fresh move of God.

The house of Israel was in the same condition when Jesus came. Under the influence of the established system, they proved their love for tradition over their love for God. When the Messiah (their ultimate focus of belief) had come, they did not receive Him because He did not fit into their preconceived ideas of what or who the Messiah would be. "He came to His own, and His own did not receive Him. But as many as received Him, to them He gave the right to become the children of God..." (Jn 1:11-12). We must not let the past interfere with our decision to respond to present truth.

Following systems rather than the anointing has institutionalized churches. If a church becomes institutionalized, it no longer fulfills the purpose for which it was founded. Institutionalization occurs when self-perpetuation becomes the major focus of an organization and it exists at the expense of the original vision.

The early Church began strong, actively demonstrating the Kingdom of God. But within a few hundred years, it became an institution—a structured organization living and existing to serve itself rather than to follow its original commission.

In churches today, the process of institutionalization occurs repeatedly. A local church reaches a point where its primary focus is no longer the vision that birthed it, but rather its existence. It succumbs to self-perpetuation at the expense of the original vision. Often this happens because people leave the church's foundation and find their satisfaction in the organization, not in Christ. Self-satisfaction replaces a desire to please God. Hypocrisy soon becomes normal behavior. People give lip service to protect the organization, but their hearts are far from God.

Labor unions are a very good illustration of this principle. They began with a group of people pulling together for the purpose of improving working conditions, the establishment of fair wages, and the procurement of benefits needed by employees. It is disheartening to see how many unions have institutionalized to such a point that they now exist at the expense of the employees they initially intended to help. Often we have seen how the political opinion of union executives has been the opposite of most of the people. How have they become so out of touch with their members? They have become institutionalized; their focus has switched from that of representing their members to the survival of the institution.

Another good example of institutionalization is found in political systems. Communism began with the teachings of Marx and Lenin, who wanted to form a government that would work for the people. Not long after the government was formed, the system itself began to arise, replacing the oppressive regime, but destroying the idealistic vision. Its new leaders concerned themselves more with how they could benefit individually than with the best interests of the people. The system spoke of the vision of their founders, yet its actions did not demonstrate that vision.

Recently, we have witnessed country after country of the former Soviet Union renouncing Communism because it became the oppressor of the people it originally sought to serve. Although we may oppose the purpose and plan of the Communist vision, it is beneficial for us to see how this same principle works in different institutions. It is the way of flesh.

The deterioration of a vision through institutionalization applies to the American government as well. Neither the Democratic nor Republican parties hold to their founding principles. Many people continue to participate in a particular party that promotes an image of its founding vision long after the original vision has diminished. We must be sensitive to the present condition of any organization to which we belong.

Even though God has called us to follow visionary people, the responsibility is always on us to discern the direction of leadership. We are accountable to God to always follow the Spirit. We must not ignore our spiritual responsibility by being confined by a system. It is our right and responsibility to know what the Spirit is saying to the Church. In Second Peter 1:12,

Peter says, "For this reason I will not be negligent to remind you always of these things, though you know them, and are established in the present truth." God's desire is to have a Church ever on the move, walking in present truth, following the anointed word of God.

The Challenge to Change

The part of our human nature that derives satisfaction from feeling like *we have arrived* is our greatest hindrance. Humans like the comfort of routine. That is why Jesus said, "And no one, having drunk old wine, immediately desires new; for he says 'The old is better' " (Lk. 5:39). In order to be a partaker of the *new wine,* we must be willing to drink that which the Lord sends, allowing change to come our way. This requires an openness to the Spirit to discern what God is speaking today. We want the new wine but we must realize that we also need *new wineskins* to hold the wine. Otherwise, the old skins will burst and we will lose all that God has for us.

If we refuse change, we will find ourselves at odds with God, who is always challenging us to change. Our refusal to change demonstrates either rebellion against God or a lack of reverence, while our willingness to change shows our respect. The psalmist declared, "God will hear, and afflict them, even He who abides from of old. Selah. Because they do not change, therefore they do not fear God. He has put forth his hands against those who were at peace with him; he has broken his covenant" (Ps. 55:19).

Isaiah 2 declares that in the last days many people shall come and say, " 'Come, and let us go up to the mountain of the Lord, to the house of the God of Jacob; He will teach us His ways, and we shall walk in His paths.' For out of Zion shall go forth the law, and the word of the Lord from Jerusalem" (Is. 2:3). God wants to establish His holy city, the Church, before the nations as a witness of the power of the God of Jacob. Jacob had a God who changed him. Even his name was changed from Jacob, which means deceiver and supplanter, to Israel, which means prince with God and man.

In order to be like Jacob, we must be willing to wrestle with God until He blesses us. Jacob refused to let go. We must be diligent to seek a blessing that leads to change. God's pattern is always the same; first He calls, then He offers a blessing or promise. It is during the process of our journey that we learn about God and experience change. This process continues until we attain the goal or purpose that God has set for our lives. This is why we must be a progressive Church, one that produces change.

When we began Mt. Zion Temple, a small group of people hearing the challenge of God, we began a journey that has continued even to today. Although thousands of people have joined us along the way and our structures have changed, our vision is the same. If we continue to seek the vision given by God, we will experience a wonderful journey learning about Him. Jesus said, "Come to Me, all you who labor and are heavy laden, and I will give you rest. Take My yoke upon you and learn from Me, for I am gentle and lowly in heart, and you will find rest for your souls. For My yoke is easy and My burden is light" (Mt. 11:28-30). What a wonderful journey God has for us. We cannot experience this journey if we cling to a system that refuses change. God is calling us to greater things. When we follow the order God has set, we will be a people always on the move, achieving God's plan for blessing and inheritance.

The church I attended as a child was really typical of many denominational churches. Over and over again different leaders would try to breathe life into the system. Oftentimes they were partially effective, but ultimately their efforts would come to a halt. Many churches are in the same position today because the leadership and organizational foundations need to change. Ministers are more concerned about their position and place of authority and how they can benefit personally from the system, rather than how they may serve. The people of the congregation also reach a place where their positions become more important than God's purpose for their individual lives. In the end, the system succeeds in quenching the move of God.

This is usually the problem in churches that remain stagnant over a long period. I am suspicious of the spiritual vitality of such churches. Most churches start small, as Mt. Zion Temple did, and the population of many communities will not support a large church, but these should be exceptions, not the rule. No matter how large a church is, it should always be progressive. Institutionalized churches are those that honor God with their lips, but have removed their hearts far from

Him. God says He will send these people a spirit of slumber to sleep and they will lose their ability to hear from God even when they desire to hear (see Rom. 11:8). This explains why Jesus came to His people and spoke to them in parables; it was not given to them to know the mysteries of God (see Mt. 13:11). They honored God with their mouths, but their hearts were far from Him.

If you find yourself in this kind of church today, you need to turn to the Lord with your whole heart. Do not stay where the judgment of God has fallen on the leadership. Find a servant of God who is hearing what the Spirit is speaking to the church and follow the anointing upon him.

If you are the leader in a situation like this, it is time to awake to God! "Awake, you who sleep, arise from the dead, and Christ will give you light" (Eph. 5:14). God is waiting for you to turn to Him with your whole heart. If you do not, the judgment of God will fall. The coming of God's judgment is a slow and deliberate process. Isaiah describes it as line upon line, precept upon precept (see Is. 28:13). This is why many people do not recognize it when it comes—until it's too late. Isaiah 29:8-14 describes the condition of the people under this judgment as follows:

> *"It shall even be as when a hungry man dreams, and look—he eats; but he awakes, and his soul is still empty; or as when a thirsty man dreams, and look—he drinks; but he awakes, and indeed*

*he is faint, and his soul still craves: so the multi-
tude of all the nations shall be, who fight against
Mount Zion." Pause and wonder! Blind yourselves and be blind! They are drunk, but not with
wine; they stagger, but not with intoxicating
drink. For the Lord has poured out on you the
spirit of deep sleep, and has closed your eyes,
namely, the prophets; and He has covered your
heads, namely, the seers. The whole vision has become to you like the words of a book that is sealed,
which men deliver to one who is literate, saying,
"Read this, please;" and he says, "I cannot, for it
is sealed." Then the book is delivered to one who
is illiterate, saying, "Read this, please;" and he
says, "I am not literate." Therefore the Lord said:
"Inasmuch as these people draw near to me with
their mouths and honor Me with their lips, but
have removed their hearts far from Me, and their
fear toward Me is taught by the commandment of
men, therefore, behold, I will again do a marvelous work among this people, a marvelous work
and a wonder; for the wisdom of their wise men
shall perish, and the understanding of their prudent men shall be hidden"* (Isaiah 29:8-14).

The Walk of Faith

God wants to restore His vision to the Church.
Proverbs 29:18 says, "Where there is no revelation [or
vision, KJV], the people cast off restraint; but happy is
he who keeps the law." He desires a people who walk in
revelation. The word *vision* in this passage speaks of

the goals set for us by God to direct us in our Christian experience. Most Christians want great faith, but they do not want to be restrained or held within a walk of faith. Hebrews 10:38 says, "Now the just shall live by faith; but if anyone draws back, My soul has no pleasure in him."

When we walk by faith, we become pilgrims and sojourners before God. First Peter 2:4-5 reads, "Coming to Him [Christ] as to a living stone, rejected indeed by men, but chosen by God and precious, you also, as living stones, are being built up a spiritual house, a holy priesthood, to offer up spiritual sacrifices acceptable to God through Jesus Christ."

God is looking for spiritual sacrifices today. We, having a living stone for our foundation, need to continue building on that foundation with living stones of divine revelation. As pilgrims and sojourners, we can stay only temporarily in one place. We need to be like Abraham, the father of our faith, who sojourned to the land of promise as to a foreign country. He dwelled in tents with Isaac and Jacob, heirs with him of the same promise, waiting for the city that had foundations, whose builder and maker was God (see Heb. 11:10).

All the great patriarchs of faith were pilgrims and sojourners who plainly declared that they sought a homeland, a better place, a heavenly country. Therefore, God was not ashamed to be called their God.

The walk of faith is a constantly-moving, ever-changing relationship with God. Unfortunately, many people do not continue the journey but choose a more stable, predictable, religious life style. My prayer is that we would awaken to new life.

Since I heard the Lord speak, "If you will go the way of the Spirit, you will possess things others have not possessed," I could never be content with earthly things again. Like Abraham, I am waiting for that heavenly city—the work of God's hand. Therefore, like Abraham, I must learn to be content dwelling in tents. I will not live in a permanent residence on this earth. Man has always wanted God to dwell in buildings, but God wants to dwell in the tents of people who are looking for a better place, a heavenly country. God is not against buildings. *Dwelling in tents* refers to the attitude of one's heart. We must continually progress in our walk with God, and not become satisfied with a place of personal contentment.

Since taking possession of our original church building, we at Mt. Zion Temple have continually been challenged to move forward. After the first year, we built an addition; after three years, we added on again. We then purchased a 52-acre site and built a new sanctuary. After one year in our new building, we added a balcony and started having two services on Sunday morning. After two years, we added again. We are constantly building.

I recall at one point, when our building program could not keep up with the growth, the Lord showed me how we could seat more people. The following week, we replaced pews with individual chairs. My sister, Jeanne, who is extremely sentimental, cried as we carried the pews out of the building. We all hated to see them go, but the work of God must always take precedence over everything else, especially our feelings and sentiments about earthly things.

The children of Israel must have felt the same way as they journeyed to the Promised Land. When the cloud or pillar of fire started to move, everyone had to prepare to leave. I'm sure it must have upset them when the trumpets began to blow, and they had to pack up everything again and move. No doubt, they complained about leaving the comforts of home to move to new surroundings. They must have longed to settle in one place; however, choosing to stay would have cost them the Promised Land as well as their ultimate comfort and security, the protection of the Lord.

In many churches and moves of God today, people refuse to let go of comfort and security when God says it's time to move. God's presence or anointing is not missed at first because their stability overrides their longing for His presence. It isn't long, though, before God's absence becomes evident. Even then, many people refuse to leave. They will encourage each other by talking about the *good old days*, but they will never admit that God's move has left them behind. At this point, their only hope is to repent and follow the fresh move of God. It seems like such a radical change when someone begins to take the initiative to move, but in reality, they are only returning to the place where they once found comfort: the presence of God.

When Jesus came, His people were in this same complacent condition. They were not only believers of the religious system; they were also captives of it. When Jesus tried to reveal God to them in a new way, the system was more important to them than the God it was intended to serve.

When Jesus met the woman at the well in John 4, she questioned Him about the system. "Our fathers worshiped on this mountain, and you Jews say that in Jerusalem is the place where one ought to worship" (Jn. 4:20). Jesus, the long-awaited Messiah, was speaking to her and she did not know Him. Jesus responded by saying, "You worship what you do not know; we know what we worship, for salvation is of the Jews. But the hour is coming, and now is, when the true worshipers will worship the Father in spirit and truth..." (Jn 4:22-23). He was telling her that the Jews at one time knew whom they worshiped, but had lost their focus because of the system. Many churches have fallen under this type of bondage.

We must always remember that God, our Father, is a Spirit. If we desire to meet with Him, we must be willing to do it on His terms, for He has proven Himself willing to meet us. The Scriptures say that God became flesh and dwelt among us so that we could see Him as He is (see Jn. 1:14). He gave us His Spirit so that we could approach Him. This is only possible in the spiritual realm.

We must not remain complacent and comfortable in any system; we must seek for full revelation of the Father. As we progress on this journey, we must lay aside the old and pick up the new. In the Father's house, we must continually walk the way of Spirit, for He is seeking such to worship Him (see Jn. 4:23).

Chapter 3

A House of Wisdom

Before God ever begins a work of ministry, He raises up a messenger. God then builds everything around the anointed word that proceeds from His messenger. When we study Scripture, we see how most Bible narratives revolve around the calling and preparation of a person God has called to lead His work.

A good example of this pattern is Abraham, the father of our faith. It continues with Abraham's sons to Moses, then to the judges following the entrance into the Promised Land. Some people would prefer to view this as strictly an Old Testament principle. However, in the Book of Acts, we see this pattern continued with the call of Paul, the apostle to the Gentiles.

When we fail to see the continuity of the work of God throughout the Old and the New Testaments, we limit our understanding and miss a great part of the plan and purpose of God. The call and preparation of the messenger is an important aspect of God's work in the Church. If the Church follows the messenger raised up by God, it will not only see the planting of the Word, but also experience the harvest of the fruit God is looking for in the earth.

Living Out the Word

When the Lord called me, the word He most prominently placed in my spirit was given to me during a special time of seeking Him. God said, "I will make you a vessel of the new wine, and I will give you a people that out of their midst shall flow the wine of the Lord...multiplication and increase...multiplication and increase." I understood that God wanted to accomplish a work in the people, but I had not yet realized the profound work that God wanted to accomplish in me.

Too many messengers tell people what God expects of them without realizing their responsibility to demonstrate the word by their own lives. When Jesus, the Author and Finisher of our faith, came to earth, He came as One with a message. However, the real message was not what He spoke, but rather the harmony of that word and the way He lived. If God has a message for you to speak, He has a life for you to live.

Often ministers say, "Don't look at me; look to Jesus." They use this important defense today especially when so many spiritual leaders have fallen. To the average Christian, this statement seems very spiritual and it always gets a hearty "Amen!" from the people. However, God's Word teaches us differently. Paul told the Corinthians, when there was confusion about leadership in the church, to "imitate me, just as I also imitate Christ." He declared that the seal of his apostleship was the work that had been accomplished in the people (see 1 Cor. 9:2).

We have strayed far from this precious biblical truth, so it's no wonder that the integrity of our leadership is so poor. We must return to the biblical pattern of emulating leaders. Then we will have true elders in the house of God.

In Acts 3, when Peter and John approached the lame man at the gate called Beautiful, they were not afraid to say, "Look at us." When the man's eyes were fixed on him, Peter said, "Silver and gold I do not have [in other words, he had nothing of himself], but what I do have I give you: In the name of Jesus Christ of Nazareth, rise up and walk" (Acts 3:6). The lame man left leaping and praising God, and multitudes of people witnessed the power of God resident in the disciples. God reveals His glory through His vessels. We must see as well that the disciples did not boast in themselves, but in the power of God. The power of God remains a prominent emphasis and the vessels reveal who they are in God.

A Crisis of Leadership

Today, Western society is facing a real crisis because of a lack of leadership. Why? First, we no longer want to honor leadership; second, we don't require that leaders earn the honor bestowed upon them; and third, the humanist influence of socialism presents a strong resistance to authority structures and with this, a loss of leadership. The generation of the 1960's and 70's especially resisted all types of authority structures; therefore, today we are reaping the fruit of our errors.

In what were once considered to be primitive societies, leadership was based on the desire to be led by the wisest member of the society. This is the reason elders played a prominent role. The elders lived long enough to not only learn, but also experience wisdom, the result of knowledge. Wisdom is not just an accumulation of knowledge, but rather knowledge proven by practice.

In our society, respect and attention is not given to a person based upon his wisdom, but upon his education. The more education a person has, the more respect he receives from his peers. The Bible says a person can be "always learning and never able to come to the knowledge of the truth" (2 Tim. 3:7).

The biblical model of leadership is to follow those who have acquired more than head knowledge. Experience that displays true wisdom will have a demonstration of practical fruit. That is why the Bible says, "Therefore by their fruits you will know them" (Mt. 7:20). A person can be very articulate, well educated, and persuasive, yet can lead people to the pits of hell. We need wisdom, especially when in the house of God. You have a right to and must look for the fruit of a leader's message in his life and in the lives of those around him.

Training Leaders

Appointment and ordination in the Church should not come from man's initiative or preference. It should be a desire to recognize those whom God has called and ordained. Credentials for ministry are not simply pieces of paper issued by religious organizations, but are to be the recognition of the fruit evident in a person's life and service. It's not that we shouldn't have the legal and structural organizations in place; we just need to follow biblical principles when choosing leaders. Instead, churches have followed the lead of the world in training leaders in educational establishments rather than in local churches.

Paul wrote to Timothy so that he, the younger man, would know how to conduct himself in the house of God, which is the pillar and ground of truth. God has ordained that the saints be equipped through the headship ministries listed in Ephesians 4. How can leadership in the Church be balanced and mature if we follow the principles of the world rather than the principles of God?

The Church must rise up as an example to the world, setting a standard for the training of leaders. God said that we are to be the head and not the tail (see Deut. 28:13). Western society once followed a form of apprenticeship in training. Fathers or elders taught their particular skills or trades to their sons who in turn taught their sons. This type of training was based on scriptural concepts, and for this reason America became a great and prosperous nation. However, we are beginning to see a lack of strong leadership as well as a breakdown in our educational and training systems today. We need to reexamine our direction for preparing leadership and ensure that it follows the principles of the Word.

This pattern is exemplified in the life of Paul. He had a very dramatic conversion, one that could easily lead to a full-time speaking ministry in our day. However, when Paul went to the established church, people didn't want to have anything to do with him because his ministry was not proven. The first aspect of his training was his personal communion with God, which is essential for all who aspire to be used of God.

Paul's experience was out of the ordinary because of the great call of God on his life—as the apostle to the Gentile church—yet he had to submit to the Church and follow a pattern of apprenticeship before he could be fully released into ministry. When the Church was afraid to receive Paul, Barnabas took him under his wing. Together they ministered in the city of Antioch and established a church there. It was that local body that laid hands on them, sending them out to fulfill their call as apostles to the Body of Christ. They had submitted to the church and had trained under the elders, putting into practice the principles the Lord had instilled in them. They were then able to go forth bearing the fruit of their message, establishing a foundational base for ministry.

Relationship Authority

When the Lord first gave me the message for my ministry, I preached it to our small group of beginners, most of who, with a few exceptions, were relatively new to the faith. As I preached the word, I began establishing myself as a messenger before them. The word God had placed in my spirit was now under close observation. Everything I preached would have to be demonstrated before this group of people. It's one thing to dream, but it's another thing altogether to see that dream come to pass. God will always be faithful to do His part. The question is, will we be faithful to do our part?

The man of God must prove himself faithful, which is the real test of stewardship. If we are faithful in the little things, God will reward us with greater things. Little by little, this word worked in me and through me. Ephesians 3:20 says, "Now to Him who is able to do exceedingly abundantly above all that we ask or think, according to the power that works in us." As the power works in and through us, it becomes more evident to those around us. The seal of our ministry is the fruit we produce.

A return to scriptural training and ordination procedures will also restore the important structural foundation of relationship. When Paul wrote to the Corinthian church about their leadership crisis, the reason he had such authority over them was because of the relationship he had established with them. Paul was the father of the Corinthian church. He said, "For though you might have ten thousand instructors in Christ, yet you do not have many fathers..." (1 Cor. 4:15).

Relationship was the basis of Paul's authority. When Jesus founded the Church, He used men whom He had carefully trained and built strong relationships with. Authority grounded in relationship has been sadly lacking in the Church and has caused many misunderstandings. Paul admonished the Corinthians to be open to various ministries of the day, but also to recognize that a place of authority in ministry should be reserved for those with whom they've had a spiritual relationship.

Relationship is so important in determining authority because we are instructed to judge one another by our fruit. Jesus warned us that wolves would come to us in sheep's clothing (see Mt. 7:15). The way to judge sheep and wolves is to examine what they do, or their fruit. Jesus also said, "Even so, every good tree bears good fruit, but a bad tree bears bad fruit" (Mt. 7:17).

In order to be fruit inspectors, we need to live in an environment where we can see each other closely. Current church leadership scandals are good cases in point. Many people put their trust and spiritual welfare into the hands of men whom those closest to them know are not spiritually mature enough to handle the pressures of a fast-growing ministry. Television and other media ministries can be spiritually uplifting, but by no means replace the role of the local church. That is why we must apply time-proven methods taught in the Word of God to our technologically-advanced society. Paul preached that we are to receive from all ministries, but only to entrust our lives to someone based on accountability and relationship.

When we build relationships in the Body of Christ, whether with ministry or lay people, we should let what we know personally about them be our guide in judging their ministry. First Timothy 5:19 states, "Do not receive an accusation against an elder except from two or three witnesses." People who do not personally know an individual have no right to make an accusation against them without regarding the fruit of their labor.

We should not listen to accusations about someone we're acquainted with, especially when that accusation goes against everything we know about that person. Paul told the Corinthian church that they were the seal of his apostleship and the proof of his credentials for ministry (see 1 Cor. 9:2). Often we hear complaints about what someone is or is not doing for God when the accuser has little to show himself. Let's be fruit inspectors!

The most significant part of the testing we experience when God is developing our characters for ministry, happens through relationships. When a person begins in ministry, his authority comes from the relationship he has built with the people he is ministering to. Most of the people in our church did not know me personally and had to establish relationship with me. They had to learn to trust me as a person before I could fully minister to them as a pastor.

As I lived a godly life before them, their confidence in my gifting and character grew. Many people, without realizing it, tested that relationship. I especially remember one young man who came to our church. He had been invited to church by a friend. He was reluctant about coming, but he wanted to prove that church people were hypocrites. He even put God to the test by saying that he wasn't going to stay if the preacher didn't speak about love. God was faithful to give me a message on love and the word pricked his heart, but he wanted and needed more than just a message about love—he needed to experience it.

It wasn't long before he started stopping by my home to ask about the Lord. Very late one night, after talking for hours, he gave his life to the Lord. He was so receptive to the Word that he didn't want to wait to be baptized. That night, we went over to the church and I baptized him. Today, 11 years later, he is still at Mt. Zion Temple, growing in the grace of God.

The concept of relationship and authority is an important truth that needs to be instituted in denominational structures. Often no provision is made for relationship authority. The structure is strictly built upon political policy. Many times regional leaders are called to deal with local ministry matters when they've had no relationship at all with those concerned. We have come far from God's original plan for the Church. Building our patterns of authority on relationship allows flexibility for change based upon the word God gave to the appointed messenger.

The entire structure is to be built on the foundation Jesus spoke of to Peter—a living, revealed word—so the Body can move in harmony with the anointing of the Holy Spirit. We need to restructure some of our organizations to reemphasize relationship structures, not political ones. Most denominational structures can trace their roots back to a time when relationship was the emphasis of its founders.

When I speak of relationship authority, I don't mean just knowing a person. I mean knowing their anointing and gifting. Paul had a relationship with all the churches that he founded, but time constraints (especially with early modes of travel) did not allow him time to build personal, intimate relationships. People in various churches knew his anointing and gifting. If we only know one another on a personal level, we severely limit God.

The Discipleship Movement in the 1970's understood the need for relationship authority, but the entire structure was built on men, not on their anointing. The result was the move of God being cut off because of overly-structured legalism. To grow in God, we do not draw from a person individually, but from his anointing.

For example, Mt. Zion Temple now numbers in the multiplied hundreds. My personal ability to reach people is limited to just a small group. The anointed word going forth, however, can reach every person in the congregation. I can be aware of their needs, by the Spirit, without really knowing them individually. People leave our services asking if I've been overhearing their conversations or talking to their friends or family. They know me by the word I preach and the life

I live before them. I know them by the anointing of the Holy Spirit.

In this way, my ministry is not confined to my human knowledge of individual situations, but has a far greater impact because of the gifting and anointing of the Spirit. Jeremiah spoke of this when he said that in the new covenant, no one would have to teach his neighbor to know the Lord, "for they all shall know Me, from the least of them to the greatest of them..." (Jer. 31:34).

Sometimes an anointed leader can father many people in his congregation, and even other ministries, because of the anointing upon his life. Although people may not witness the personal fruit of the messenger, they can witness the fruit of his message in their lives.

As long as a church is training and ordaining ministry to tend to the needs of the flock, there are no limitations to its size. If the leader's gifting is apostolic, his influence can extend beyond the local church to minister to other churches or ministries and by using modern methods of communication, the word can reach multitudes. This was demonstrated by Paul when he wrote letters to the early churches. He started or established churches and then appointed leaders over them. These leaders then exercised oversight while under Paul's influence. The governing authority of each church was local—not transcontinental.

Wanted: Wise Leadership

The Book of Judges records how God appointed leadership by placing His anointing on someone in the midst of His people. When that individual died, the children of Israel would then have to seek out another as God's anointed messenger or deliverer. Once they found the one anointed of God, the structure of authority would fall into place around that person. The children of Israel became weary of having to look for God's leaders, for God rarely placed His anointed where they expected. They began asking God for a king instead, and God allowed them to have one.

We today are no different than the children of Israel—we find it easier to trust an existing structure rather than to seek the anointed of God and totally trust Him. Because it's easier, we substitute kings for prophets. We appoint leadership based on theological degrees, years of service or experience, religious or family connections, etc., rather than on the sovereign appointment of the Holy Spirit.

The New Testament believer, with the life of Christ as his example, understands that God desires someone whose character and life style is consistent to the gifting and talents that the Lord has given. This is the kind of leadership that the Father wants to demonstrate in His house and to the world.

Solomon declares that wisdom calls aloud; she raises her voice in the open squares and the openings of the gates to the city. She cries out to the simple ones to understand and for fools to have an understanding heart. Wisdom says, "Listen and I will speak excellent things. Blessed is the man who listens to me, for whoever finds me finds life and obtains favor from God; but he who sins against me wrongs his own soul. All those who hate me, love death." (See Proverbs 8:32-36.) God wants to display His wisdom to the world, for His wisdom will become their source of life.

In the garden of Eden, man chose to eat of the tree of the knowledge of good and evil rather than the tree of life. The tree of life was nothing less than the tree of wisdom. Proverbs 3:13-18 says:

Happy is the man who finds wisdom, and the man who gains understanding; for her proceeds are better than the profits of silver, and her gain than fine gold. She is more precious than rubies, and all the things you may desire cannot compare with her. Length of days is in her right hand, in her left hand riches and honor. Her ways are ways of pleasantness, and all her paths are peace. She is a tree of life to those who take hold of her, and happy are all who retain her (Proverbs 3:13-18).

We need a demonstration of wisdom in our Father's house. Those who seek to minister life must also become a tree of life to the world. The fruit of the righteous is a tree of life. In Revelation 22:1-2, John saw a tree whose leaves were healing for the nations. The tree drew its life from the stream of life that flowed from the throne of God. This tree symbolizes the blessed seed of Abraham, which God promised to be a blessing to all the nations of the earth. Ezekiel saw this same vision as many trees, showing the importance of the Church (see Ezek. 47).

Those of us who have experienced and enjoyed the Pentecostal and Charismatic flow of that river need to realize that the Father is now asking us to be trees planted by that river of living water. We should no longer just be drinking from that stream, but should be trees planted in God's wisdom, trees that John said would be healing for the nations. The Husbandman of the earth, who brings the early and latter rain, patiently watches for that fruit.

Wisdom is demonstrated by our keeping God's commandments. The fear of the Lord is the beginning of wisdom and this is our first step on the path of life. As we fear the Lord and keep His commandments, we are to trust Him with all our hearts and not depend upon our own understanding. In all our ways, we are to acknowledge Him and He will direct our paths. We cannot be wise in our own eyes, but we must fear the Lord and depart from evil. (See Proverbs 3:5-7.)

We must then honor God with our possessions and the firstfruits of our increase. As we continue to walk, the words from God will bring instruction and correction. If we will understand that these words are the products of God's love and not despise them, we will become a living demonstration of the Father's wisdom and happiness and life will be our end.

Today, as we sit in the ash heaps of the failures of many of our church leaders, we must realize the need to demonstrate wisdom to the world. The failures of men should not lower our expectations of the people of God; instead they should only encourage us to provide a greater witness to the earth. We must accept this challenge and give people something to see instead of trying to hide and hoping that they won't see us and be disappointed. Like Peter and John, I want us to declare, "Look on us; we have something that will heal your affliction."

Chapter 4

A House
of Empowerment

When someone receives a vision or word from the
Lord for ministry, he continually anticipates the fulfillment of that word. He who has received faith from the
imparted word begins a journey like Abraham's; he
looks for the end result of his faith—the promised possession. However, anyone who has had a real meeting
with God yearns for another. It's no wonder that some
in the early Church only sought for His return. What
could be more appealing than to be forever in His
presence?

Paul himself, though highly motivated to preach
the gospel, said he was caught between the intense
desire to be in God's presence and the desire to fulfill

his ministry on earth. He finally settled in his spirit that he needed to remain for the benefit of those he was called to minister to (see Phil. 1). Like Paul, we too are caught between the desire to depart from this life to be with the Lord or to stay and do what we are called to do. It is this dilemma that the Church must resolve: We want to escape the toil of the Christian life for the blessing of His presence, or we walk in works and forget His presence. David said, "My foot stands in an even place; in the congregations I will bless the Lord" (Ps. 26:12).

When Jesus ascended, it was promised that He would return the same way, in clouds of glory (see Acts 1:9-11). Paul calls this the *blessed hope* of the Church. With great anticipation we await His return in fulfillment of His promise, yet we must understand that when He comes, He is expecting us to have accomplished something while He was gone.

In the same way, when we receive a word of promise about our lives or ministries, we are always left with great anticipation. Our most meaningful experiences or meetings with God occur when a seed of promise has been planted in our spirits. Even when we begin to see the fulfillment of the vision, a part of us continually looks for another meeting with God. This is only natural for those who love the Lord, for being in His presence is more precious than anything He could ever give. Therefore, we always yearn for another experience with Him. At the same time, we desire fulfillment of the commission or vision He has already given to us.

Sometimes when we receive a vision from God, it becomes so real to us that we feel it's within our immediate reach. Because we always want instant results and are constantly struggling with time, we don't have the patience to wait. The disciples must have felt this way as Jesus ministered with them; they always looked for the immediate fulfillment of the word and the promise of the Kingdom.

Our desire for a continual intimate relationship with God and our impatience to wait for results can hinder us from facing the work at hand. The relationship-oriented person wants to forget the toil of everyday life and just stay before the Lord in prayer. The works-oriented person thrives on quick results and accomplishments. We must maintain the important balance between our relationship with God and our need to work for Him. Isaiah 1:19-20 says, "If you are willing and obedient, you shall eat the good of the land; but if you refuse and rebel, you shall be devoured by the sword...." When we receive and believe the word God has given, we need to begin to work the land of our inheritance.

Receiving the Inheritance

Soon after the children of Israel arrived at the threshold of the Promised Land after crossing the Jordan River, they experienced a tremendous change. As they entered the land and began to eat the fruit, the manna from Heaven ceased to fall. It was time to eat of the land, and in order to do so, they had to work. They probably thought they would have plenty when they entered the Promised Land; however, this was not so. When the promise came, it was only the means to obtain their food. The actual food came from how they utilized the land after they had received it.

Often we seek God for things we are not in a position to handle. For this reason, God works ever so gently and patiently with us until we can fully understand and receive the promise He has for us. Then the question is, what will we do with what the Lord has placed in our hands?

Hebrews 11:6 says, "But without faith it is impossible to please Him, for he who comes to God must believe that He is, and that He is a rewarder of those who diligently seek Him." A person of faith must be motivated by the desire to please God just because He is God. We must believe that God is a rewarder of those who seek Him. This implies seeking Him and believing in His promises like all the heroes of faith listed did.

The promise of God is not an elective. When the children of Israel refused to take possession of the Promised Land after being discouraged by the reports given by ten of the spies, the sentence of death was placed upon them. God is looking for aggressive, bold, courageous people to follow Him. It is time for us to work the land and possess our inheritance.

According to Hebrews 6:11-12, we must show diligence, full assurance, and hope until the end or we will become lazy. We are to imitate those whom through faith and patience inherit the promises. God has not only called us to a relationship with Him; He has also called us to do a work for Him. The Bible emphasizes in James 2 that faith without works is dead. A walk of faith changes our characters into the likeness of God.

Just as the Lord has much patience, we too need to have much patience. Many people believe that God is in a hurry. They aggressively labor for a quick solution, which only causes them to lose their rest and make decisions based upon their goals for immediate success. Meanwhile, God is concerned with the eternal and long-term results.

Jesus shared an important parable with His disciples that addressed this problem (see Lk. 19). When He spoke the parable of the minas, or pounds, He knew that He had only a short time left and that they thought the Kingdom of God would appear immediately. The disciples did not want to be separated from Jesus, so they believed that God would exercise supernatural forces to establish the Kingdom of God on earth.

This parable speaks about a nobleman who departed to a far country to receive a kingdom, leaving his servants with equal portions of money. When he returned, he asked his servants to give an account of what they had done with their portion. They each received a reward according to how they used the money. The last servant to give an account had done nothing with what he had been given and not only missed out on a reward, but also lost the portion he had. The statement that Jesus made does not settle well in our pattern of humanistic thinking: For I say to you, that "to everyone who has will be given; and from him who does not have, even what he has will be taken away from him" (Lk. 19:26). This is the law of stewardship.

In God's Kingdom, there are no excuses that relieve us of our responsibility to labor. The servant believed he had a good excuse for hiding the money when he said he was afraid. However, the nobleman called him a wicked and lazy servant, and the servant lost all.

Citizenship in the Kingdom of God is very serious because God holds each of us accountable to use and increase our talents. It is time to make use of what the Father has placed in our hands. In Luke 19:17 it is thrilling to read what God has promised to the faithful ones, those who have multiplied what has been placed in their hands. One servant was given authority over ten cities and another over five. The key word here is *authority*. God wants to give His Church authority.

Empowerment

The Lord clearly spoke to me that He wanted the Church to be a place of empowerment. I had heard this word before, but I didn't fully understand it. The word *empowerment* has a twofold meaning. It means to give someone an ability to do something, as well as the power to do it.

This power is imparted to Christians as the gift of the Holy Spirit. Acts 1:8 says, "But you shall receive power when the Holy Spirit has come upon you...."

When you receive the Spirit of God, you are empowered for service. When Jesus ascended to Heaven, the Bible says that He gave gifts to men (see Eph. 4:8). He gives gifts to us severally, as He wills, but we all receive ability when we receive the Holy Spirit.

The power of God to salvation is another source of power that we receive (see Rom. 1:16). Paul knew firsthand about this power because of his conversion experience. He was so committed to the gospel that he took it all over the world. God has given this power to the Church collectively and to individual believers as well. It has been placed in our hands, and we are accountable for it.

When a believer supports the ministry of a local church and begins to share the burden, he releases power to his community. When the message goes forth, even as a simple testimony, the power of God is released. Revelation 12:11 says that the believer overcomes (the world, the flesh, and the devil) by the blood of the Lamb and the word of his testimony. We will also be held accountable for releasing the power of our testimonies, that which God has accomplished in our lives.

Another source of power is money. You may think you don't have enough money to do much; however, even the smallest amount of money has power to purchase something. That is why we will be held accountable for paying our tithes. Whether it be ten percent of $100 or ten percent of $10,000, the percentage that is tithed is the same. By tithing, we acknowledge what portion belongs to God and that He is our source.

The words *power* and *empowerment* are closely related, but there is a vast difference in how they are used. The word *power* implies strength, might, or force, while *empower* means to not only give power to someone, but also to give them the authority to use it. The Church needs a full understanding of empowerment in order to appreciate the work that God wants to perform.

When Jesus relayed the parable of the minas or pounds, He spoke of empowerment—the nobleman gave his servants power in the form of money. As a reward, the faithful servants were given authority over cities because they properly used their power. Power plus authority equals empowerment. God wants the Church to be a place of empowerment—not just a people with power, but a people walking in authority.

The twentieth-century Church has demonstrated power, but has sorely lacked authority. I have been involved in many prayer services where a church has cried out to God for more power, not understanding that on the Day of Pentecost, the Church was given a total infusion of all the power she could ever need. The problem is not a lack of power, but rather a lack of authority. A lot of teaching about the authority of the believer primarily deals with displays of power—not true authority.

As Jesus ministered to the multitudes, they marveled at Him because He spoke with authority (see Mt. 7:28-29). He was different from the scribes and Pharisees. They were scholars of the Word and knew every religious law, yet they demonstrated no authority in their lives. The Church today is in this condition: knowledge, ritual, and noise, but no authority.

With the serious issues and pressing problems of our day, we need all that God has for us. To produce results, we must learn to move from power into authority. The Church has been waiting for God to do something when God is wanting His Church to do something. It's time to move into the realm of real spiritual authority where God is able to delegate greater responsibility to us.

The Necessity of Work

Another concept we need to grasp is work. When the nobleman departed, he instructed the servants to do business until he returned. We need to fully understand what the words *do business* mean if we are to properly relate them to the concept of the second coming of Christ. They are from the original Greek word *pragmateuomai,* which the English word *pragmatic* is derived from. It means to busy oneself with or to occupy.

Many Christians sit idly by waiting for specific instructions or direction from the Lord. People with high and lofty goals wait for a specific opening before they, if ever, put to use the gifts God has given them. They don't stoop to do mundane chores or meet the simple needs of those around them. Only when we effectively use the power we have been given, can we walk in a higher level of experience and authority.

Hebrews 5:14 says, "But solid food [or strong meat, KJV] belongs to those who are of full age, that is, those who by reason of use have their senses exercised to discern both good and evil." The stronger, more responsible ministry waits until we have matured and developed our gifts in the lesser areas of service.

When the Lord comes to bring promotion, we may not be able to receive it if we have not properly used what God has placed in our hands. Many people have waited so long to use their gifts that they are no longer active or productive. People want to do great things for God, but do not want to do the pragmatic things necessary to bring to pass the words spoken over them. Then they accuse God of letting them down.

The second aspect of the word *pragmatic* implies a habitual or repetitious use of something. It also correlates with the word *exercise* in the Book of Hebrews. We have all heard that practice makes perfect; however, Hebrews 6:1 declares that we are not to lay again the foundations, but instructs and encourages us to go on to perfection. This portion of Scripture is often overlooked. The word *perfection* does not mean to be flawless or perfect, but to be made whole and complete. We are perfect when we totally fulfill what God has called us to be. It is time for the Church to hear the call of God to go on to perfection—and it only comes by the habitual use of the gifts God has given to us.

Just as empowerment comes through the habitual use of our gifts, excellency comes by our tending to minute details. A humorous example of this is my children and their piano lessons. Their teacher assigns exercises that will fine-tune their basic skills. Initially, they were excited and loved learning to play the piano, but now, because of the repetitious practicing, they hate it. Bonnie and I continue to encourage them. Hopefully one day, they will see the benefit of their commitment. It is really the same in our Christian walk.

Our Father, in His mercy, continues to encourage us to press forward because He knows one day we will be blessed as we master the basics of our Christian experience and move on toward perfection. It is only when we move on to maturity that we actually fulfill the purpose for which we were created. I teach candidates for ministry that if a minister fails, it is not because his gift is lacking, but because of a weakness in his character.

If we are to be imitators of those whom through faith and patience have inherited the blessings of God, then our faith must be tried. First Peter 1:6-7 says not to be grieved over the trying of our faith, for it works the patience of God into our characters, "that the genuineness of your faith, being much more precious than gold that perishes, though it is tested by fire, may be found to praise, honor, and glory at the revelation of Jesus Christ." Let the Father teach you and empower you for the task that is ahead.

When my children practice their piano lessons, it is not uncommon to hear them play songs they already know. It's easier to play a melody that they've mastered rather than practice something new and tedious. When we hear them play "Chopsticks," which is more fun than fingering techniques or scales, we tell them to get back to the lesson. They complain as we push them back on course. Christians are no different. We fix our eyes on something great that we want to accomplish and are often pulled away prematurely from the mundane and tedious to do the glorious and spectacular, until God pulls us back on course. Again, we must remind ourselves that God wants to empower us.

It is hard for us to believe that God, who holds all power in His hands, is concerned about the details of our lives. However, He does everything right and in perfect order. He demands the same from us. When God comes to us from time to time during special visitations, He rewards us according to how we've tended to the details of our work. Our faithfulness and obedience to the small tasks qualify us for promotion in the Kingdom of God.

Our Spiritual Authority

We must understand the concepts of authority and empowerment if we are to function in the realm of the Spirit. In the Book of Daniel, the archangel Michael is called the angel of God's people (see Dan. 10:21; 12:1). He is accredited with casting satan out of Heaven in Revelation 12:7-9. Jude 9 says that when Michael contended with the devil for the body of Moses, he did not bring a railing accusation against satan. In other words, he understood the need to respect even the power given to satan. How did Michael handle the situation? He spoke, "The Lord rebuke you!" He did not challenge the devil on the basis of power, but on the basis of authority. There is a big difference.

We need spiritual understanding to break and tear down the powers of darkness that control our land. Many Christians stand against the devil on the merits of their own power—only to face defeat. Why? They stood against the devil, power for power, and the devil won. We will never defeat the devil by overpowering him; his level of power far exceeds ours. To think otherwise is to be a presumptuous, self-willed, brute beast spoken of in Second Peter 2:10-12, who will soon fall victim to its own folly. The only way we can defeat satan is to use our authority.

Michael, as commander of the Lord's host, knew he was sent on a mission of God. Thus his authority was greater than satan's. He did not operate in his own angelic power, but in the authority given from God for his mission. He had total control of the situation and was able to cast satan out of Heaven, never to bring accusations of the brethren again to God (see Rev. 12:7-10).

In the Church, many immature Christians have shown off their power—only to fall as victims in the war against evil. In the parable, when the nobleman saw the way his servants faithfully handled power, he then gave them authority. Authority is not something that we demand or proclaim, but something we earn. Even Jesus Himself, the Son of God, was not given immediate empowerment.

Jesus was 30 years old when full authority was given to Him for His ministry. Jesus *increased* in stature and favor with God and with men (see Lk. 2:52). Although He had enough knowledge at 12 years old to confound the teachers of the temple, His time of ministry had not yet come. Jesus did not operate with full authority until the time appointed by His Father. Often we try to force the hand of God by moving into areas we are not ready or prepared for. Promotion will not come to the proud or the presumptuous, but to the faithful ones in the house of the Lord.

When we understand the importance of being faithful stewards in our Father's house, the character of God will be developed in us completely. We will be faithful even as our heavenly Father is faithful. Our gifts come from His grace at work in our lives, but our reward is determined by the development of the fruit of the Spirit in us.

Chapter 5

A House of Glory

In February 1980, Bonnie and I were married during a Sunday night service at church. While we were still on our honeymoon, the Spirit of the Lord began to call me to prayer. You can be sure that it was a very strong motivation from the Lord to get me alone to pray on my honeymoon. As I sought the Lord, a prophetic word began to surge through me concerning the days of ministry that were ahead. The word of the Lord was this: "I will place My glory upon you, for I want to share My glory with My people." Although I was deeply affected by this profound experience, I was also troubled about what I heard. I had always been told that when serving God, one always had to be mindful not to touch the glory—it belongs to God and to Him alone.

I shared my thoughts with the congregation about the word that the Lord had given to me, and then read Isaiah 42:8. In it God declares, "I am the Lord, that is My name; and My glory I will not give to another...." I always understood this passage to mean that God would not share His glory with anyone. To my surprise, I realized that God says He will not share it with another, *except the one mentioned in this passage.* The whole chapter speaks about the Servant of the Lord. He will not share His glory with anyone other than His Servant, His Elect One in whom His soul delights (see Is. 42:1). This passage refers first to Jesus Christ, but continues to say in the next chapter, " 'You are My witnesses,' says the Lord, 'And My servant whom I have chosen...' " (Is. 43:10). Jesus was to be the firstborn of many brethren. Romans 8:28-31 states that brethren are chosen, justified, and bound for God's glory. This is God's purpose and destiny for all of His children.

After the service, one of our members, Lolly Dye, and I were in prayer at the altar. As I prayed, the anointing of God came upon me and I began to pray in tongues. During the prayer I opened my eyes and noticed that Lolly was crying. When we had finished praying, Lolly told me that a miracle had taken place. While praying in tongues, I had actually spoken Spanish and had given her a word from the Lord about someone in her family. Other members of Lolly's family heard and understood as well. At that time I had not studied Spanish, so this experience confirmed what the Lord had been speaking to me. He also showed me how it would be fulfilled. When God used me to speak in a language I did not know and allowed Lolly to interpret, it was a sign of God's power. Yet the manifestation of the gifting in me was proof of God's also filling the vessel with His glory.

A Vessel for Glory

Whenever God allows His glory to flow through us, the purpose is twofold: It glorifies God and it glorifies the vessel. Although I hesitate to make a statement like this, I know it is true: Anyone who accomplishes great things in God knows that honor also comes to him. Religion often teaches that we are to deny the honor for fear of divine retribution, but the fact is, God delights in blessing His servants. God will put His glory upon us as long as we acknowledge Him as the source of all the glory. Romans 8:30-31 says, "Moreover whom He predestined, these He also called; whom He called, these He also justified; and whom He justified, these He also glorified. ...If God is for us, who can be against us?" There is no doubt in my mind that God is, indeed, for us. What a great salvation God has for those who love Him. First Corinthians 2:9 says, "But as it is written: 'Eye has not seen, nor ear heard, nor have entered into the heart of man, the things which God has prepared for those who love Him.' "

We can know the purpose and plan of God for our lives by the power of the Holy Spirit within us. We need to allow God to open our eyes to the hope of His calling and to the riches of the glory of Christ's inheritance in the saints (see Eph. 1:18).

When we really begin to see the richness of that inheritance, we will surrender our lives to fulfill that for which we are called. God has manifested His glory through me many times. Each time, because of His glory filling me, I was honored before men. On the surface this seems to give place to personal exaltation, but we must be willing to accept God's bestowing of glory upon us in order for the full plan of God to be demonstrated in the earth. We are destined to glory, but our motivation must never be to seek it for ourselves. Our pursuit must always be to glorify God.

This pattern is demonstrated in the life of Moses as well. Moses, like no one other than Jesus Christ, manifested the glory of God in the earth. The manifestation was so great that the children of Israel were afraid to look directly at Moses because his face shone with God's glory (see Ex. 34:29-30). Yet, by reading the Scriptures, we can discover what really motivated Moses.

After the incident concerning the golden calf, as the children of Israel were camped in the wilderness, Moses pitched a tent far from the camp to meet with God. As Moses talked with God about the journey to the Promised Land, God said that His presence would not go with the children of Israel because of their sin; His presence would only go with Moses. Moses immediately responded, "If Your Presence does not go with us, do not bring us up from here" (Ex. 33:15). Moses did not want to enter into the inheritance if the children of Israel did not have God's presence in their midst. Moses exemplifies a leader with a servant's heart. We need leaders in the Church today who are God-seekers and not self-seekers. Moses is an excellent example of a leader blessed by God. He loved God and loved the people, so God had great things prepared for him.

A Personal Relationship

Although the Lord has done many supernatural things through me, when I think of my relationship with Him, I realize that I loved God long before He ever did anything miraculous for me. I fell in love with Him, and I found out that I was His concern. We must be aware that God not only watches the *big* things we do, but also the *small* things. Often those seemingly insignificant things we feel are unimportant to God are the very things God uses to judge our hearts. He is the God who looks upon the heart.

Moses had a pure heart and a true love for God, so God in turn talked with Moses face to face as a man would talk with a friend. However, there is a prerequisite to an intimate relationship with God. As Jesus was preparing to leave this earth, He shared with His disciples the most personal thoughts of His heart—thoughts that others were not able to hear. He said to them, "No longer do I call you servants, for a servant does not know what his master is doing; but I have called you friends, for all things that I have heard from My Father I have made known to you" (Jn. 15:15). Jesus wanted a friendship relationship with His disciples. He wanted to share with them what His Father had spoken to Him.

We know that Moses and Abraham had close friendships with God, but we must understand that God also wants to have this kind of relationship with us. Building a friendship with Him should be a natural part of our spiritual development. Many people sing the old hymn, *What a Friend We Have in Jesus*, but rarely walk in that type of relationship. They do not understand that friendship succeeds a servant relationship. Before the disciples could be the friends of Jesus, they first had to be His servants.

Being a Servant

Remember, when God says He will share His glory, it will be with the servant He has chosen. It is ironic that in the Kingdom of God, the servant is the leader. He who desires to be first must be a servant of all (see Mk. 9:35). As we seek the blessings of God, we continue on a step-by-step process and build our relationship with Him. With maturity comes added responsibility.

Even when God has appointed a great inheritance for us, it will be withheld from us until we have matured. Galatians 4:1-2 says, "...the heir, as long as he is a child, does not differ at all from a slave [or servant], though he is master of all, but is under guardians and stewards until the time appointed by the father." We begin our relationship in our Father's house, serving and preparing for our inheritance, which will be given at an appointed time. In our heavenly Father's house, we must provide an environment where sons can develop and mature until the appointed hour of inheritance.

The attributes of a true servant of God are listed in Isaiah 42. "Behold! My Servant whom I uphold, My Elect One in whom My soul delights! I have put My

Spirit upon Him; He will bring forth justice to the Gentiles. He will not cry out, nor raise His voice, nor cause His voice to be heard in the street" (Is. 42:1-2). The servant does not seek personal recognition. Jesus, our perfect example, never boasted about His power or what He could do. Whenever someone experienced great blessing from His ministry, Jesus often told them to keep it a secret (i.e., Mt. 8:4). When we accomplish something great, we want to run and tell everyone. Jesus never pursued selfish ambition. He sought only to bring glory to His Father. People who seek personal glory will never experience the glory of God.

Isaiah 42:3 continues to say, "A bruised reed He will not break, and smoking flax He will not quench; He will bring forth justice for truth." The servant of the Lord is gentle. Paul, writing to Timothy, says, "And a servant of the Lord must not quarrel but be gentle to all, able to teach, patient, in humility correcting those who are in opposition, if God perhaps will grant them repentance, so that they may know the truth" (2 Tim. 2:24-25).

A contentious person is one who tries to convince everyone that his view is correct or true. A servant, on the other hand, knows he serves his master and is not personally offended when others do not agree or cooperate with him. Samuel cried out to God because the people had rejected him as their leader in favor of a king. God instructed Samuel not to be disheartened because the people were not rejecting him; they were rejecting God (see 1 Sam. 8:7). Having put this into proper perspective, Samuel was able to stand before the people, disregarding his personal feelings, and do what God had asked him to do.

Finally, Isaiah 42:4 says, "He [the servant] will not fail nor be discouraged, till He has established justice in the earth...." Although the servant of the Lord is meek, not seeking personal glory or forcing the hand of the people, he most certainly is not weak. His personal character is strong; he will patiently endure any circumstance until the will of his master has been accomplished. Many times we perceive meek people to be weak. Jesus, our ultimate example of a servant, was quite the contrary. He displayed His true meekness as He faced the cross. He remained steadfast, even when the multitude that once adored Him hurled accusations at Him. Whether the crowds praised or cursed Him, He persevered and reacted no differently because His purpose was to do the will of the Father.

Being a Friend

When the Lord first gave me the vision of the ministry of Mt. Zion Temple, I thought it would be fulfilled immediately. Yet, as God revealed my need for personal growth, I began to see that God was developing the character of a servant in me. The attributes of a servant came quickly to me, but then the Lord began to show me my need to move into the next realm: friendship with Him.

I wasn't comfortable with the thought of God sharing His glory with me because I felt it was contrary to my personality and character. God then had to remind

me of the first part of this passage in Isaiah, "My servant whom I uphold, My Elect One in whom My soul
delights..." (Is. 42:1). It's hard for us to accept, but God
knows us better than we know ourselves. In the garden
of Gethsemane, in the presence of the Father, Jesus
had to face His fears and struggle with the choices He
had to make. We must present ourselves to God in
order to receive His grace to go on. Remember that God
knew us when He called us and sovereignly chose us.
He knows that we can make it, with His help.

Moses was a servant long before he ever met God
face to face and became His friend. When he descended
the mountain and the children of Israel were worship-
ing the golden calf, God told Moses that He was going
to consume or destroy them and raise up a new nation
(see Ex. 32:10). If Moses had not had the heart of a true
servant, he could have agreed to allow God to kill all
the Israelites. His reaction proved that he was a servant. He pleaded with the Lord to relent from harming
them. Moses told God that if He would not forgive
them, to also blot his name out of the Book (see Ex.
32:11,32).

Few ministers are so sold out to God that they
would surrender personal access to the Promised Land
for the people's sake. In John 15:12-13, Jesus said,
"This is My commandment, that you love one another
as I have loved you. Greater love has no one than this,
than to lay down one's life for his friends." God wants
us to meditate on this principle and consciously examine our true motives. The Father is seeking leaders

who care as much for His people as He does. A true servant sacrifices everything for the people, God's inheritance. God is tired of those who lord over His
heritage and, if necessary, He will scatter the sheep to
deliver them from such rulers (see Ezek. 34).

After you have proven yourself to be a faithful servant, you are ready to develop a friendship with Him.
Unlike a servant, a friend knows what the Master is
doing. A friend also has a right to ask things. In John
15:16, Jesus told His disciples, "You did not choose Me,
but I chose you and appointed you that you should go
and bear fruit, and that your fruit should remain, that
whatever you ask the Father in My name He may give
you." With this friendship comes great authority—an
authority that places us right in the center of God's
purpose for the earth.

After Moses proved himself to be a servant, he became the friend of God. In Exodus 33:17, God told
Moses, "I will also do this thing that you have spoken
[which was to allow God's presence to go with the entire nation]; for you have found grace in My sight, and
I know you by name." Because of the intimacy of their
relationship, Moses did not hesitate to say to God,
"Please show me Your glory" (Ex. 33:18). In response,
God said this:

> ..."I will make all My goodness pass before you,
> and I will proclaim the name of the Lord before
> you. I will be gracious to whom I will be gracious,
> and I will have compassion on whom I will have
> compassion." But He said, "You cannot see My

face; for no man shall see Me, and live" (Exodus 33:19-20).

God placed Moses in the cleft of the rock as He passed by. Because of their friendship, Moses saw the glory of God.

The Two Aspects to Glory

Two important aspects of God's glory are illustrated in this encounter between Moses and God. The first is the obvious, "glitter glory," the mystical overwhelming presence of an almighty God. This was the same type of glory that shone from Moses' face and caused the people to be afraid to look at him. This shining glory gives only a glimpse of God. But Moses knew God's glory was much greater than this.

The children of Israel were acquainted with the acts of God, but Moses knew His ways (see Ps. 103:7). Moses was privileged to catch a glimpse of the magnificence of God, but even more, to actually know Him. This, of course, is the greatest part of God's glory—not what He can do but who He is. This is the reason God allowed His goodness, mercy, and compassion to pass before Moses. Too many people only seek the surface or "glitter glory" and never discover the true glory of God: knowing Him personally. This has been a pitfall in the Charismatic Movement. With a renewed emphasis on the power of the Holy Spirit, with the gifts and the presence of God that we've grown accustomed to in our praise services, it is possible that we have lost sight of the real purpose of our pursuit, which is to know Him as He is (see Phil. 3:10). According to Hebrews 11:6, we must believe that He is, and that He is a rewarder of those who diligently seek Him. Even Abraham wasn't just seeking a blessing; he was looking for a city with foundations whose builder and maker was God (see Heb. 11:10).

Second Corinthians 3:7-8 says that in the New Covenant, a glory will be revealed, a glory greater than the glory revealed through Moses. The glory of Moses faded over time, but the glory revealed in the New Covenant will not fade away. This glory is revealed in the person of Jesus Christ, the express image of God (see Heb. 1:3). Jesus personifies the glory revealed to Moses. Yet, what was withheld from Moses is now revealed to us through Jesus Christ; we can truly look on God and live. "And...we beheld His glory," John declared, "the glory as of the only begotten of the Father, full of grace and truth" (Jn. 1:14). Jesus embodied the revelation of the name and character of God.

Even to today, many moves of God have only focussed on the fading "glitter glory." When we begin to see God as He is, we will begin to see the reality of His power as never before. We will also experience a greater increase in our faith. Most people believe God can do anything, yet they never fully expect that He will. Remember the parable of the talents? The servant who did not produce anything was hindered by his distorted perception of his master. Our misunderstanding of God paralyzes us with fear, which prevents us from serving Him effectively. First John 4:18 says, "There is no fear in love; but perfect love casts out fear, because fear involves torment...." Fear is a primary hindrance to entering into the promises of God. We need to know Him.

Spreading the Glory

As our relationship with God matures, we begin to bear His glory. When Moses bore the glory of God before the children of Israel, they could not look upon him because their hearts were hard. Their eyes were blinded as if by a veil, but in Christ the veil is taken away. (See Second Corinthians 3:12-16.) Turning to God brings us directly into the flow of the Spirit. We have the liberty to behold the face and person of God. As we behold Him unveiled before us, we are transformed into His image from glory to glory. Then we can fulfill the desire of the Father to be epistles or letters read of all men.

Prophecy declares that the knowledge of the glory of the Lord will cover the earth as the waters cover the sea (see Hab. 2:14). We are that covering; we reveal who God is to our generation. This is my earnest desire as an individual, and one that I believe must be demonstrated by the local church in every community. It is time for the Church to quit basking in the "glitter glory" and to go on to the ultimate glory of God, which is revealed by knowing Him. As we walk in close relationship with God, truly these signs will follow: we will lay hands on the sick and they will recover; we will cast out demons; we will speak with new tongues; we will take up serpents; and if we drink any deadly thing, it will not hurt us (see Mk. 16:17-18).

Our relationship with Him will reveal the full glory of God, both in the operation of our gifting and in the revelation of His character. Second Corinthians 3:2-3 says, "You are our epistle written in our hearts, known and read by all men; clearly you are an epistle of Christ, ministered by us, written not with ink but by the Spirit of the living God, not on tablets of stone but on tablets of flesh, that is, of the heart." In this New Covenant, God's law will be written upon the fleshly tablets of our hearts. Only when we have an intimate relationship with God can our lives reflect the very nature and character of God.

Second Corinthians 3:17 tells us that where the Spirit of the Lord is, there is liberty. Many in the Pentecostal and Charismatic Movements have used this passage to justify an order of service where people believe the move of the Holy Spirit gives everyone the right to do whatever they want or feel. Instead, Paul is saying that the liberty of the Spirit gives us the freedom not only to turn to God, but also to become more like Him. This is why Paul continued in verse 18, "But we all, with unveiled face, beholding as in a mirror the glory of the Lord, are being transformed into the same image from glory to glory, just as by the Spirit of the Lord."

When we, like Moses, experience the true glory of His character and not just the "glitter glory", we will indeed begin to manifest God's glory, character, and power to our generation. This is the whole purpose of our calling and election. Romans 8:29-30 says:

For whom He foreknew, He also predestined to be conformed to the image of His Son, that He might be the firstborn among many brethren. Moreover, whom He predestined, these He also called; whom He called, these He also justified; and whom He justified, these He also glorified.

God predestined and called you to be a revealed son. Before you can ever walk as a son, you must be established as the elect and chosen servant walking in intimate fellowship with Him. Today, God's desire is to reveal His abiding glory in us, the glory of His character revealed in people who have had a personal encounter with Him.

Chapter 6

A House of Sons

Once we have matured in our walk with God beyond the servant stage to the friendship stage, there is another level to attain. This is the full-heir son, the most intimate level of relationship—and God wants to bring the entire Body of Christ to this level today. However, God always starts with His appointed leaders. Remember, Galatians 4:1-2 says, "...the heir, as long as he is a child, does not differ at all from a slave, though he is master of all, but is under guardians and stewards until the time appointed by the father." I sense the Holy Spirit signifying that this is the appointed time for the Church to go on to maturity. The Spirit is calling us to go further, beyond any previous level of experience. Romans 8 tells how the whole of creation groans and travails together for the revelation or manifestation of the sons of God in the earth. When we receive the Holy Spirit, that Spirit also groans in us for the fulfillment of that same purpose. If you will listen with your heart, you will hear what the Spirit is speaking to the Church.

Going on to Perfection

The Spirit is groaning for the fulfillment of God's command to go on to perfection or maturity. A proper foundation prepares and enables us to go on. The word *perfect* means to be complete, whole, entire— everything God wants us to be. I may never be everything that people want me to be, but I must believe that I can be everything God wants me to be. The cross offered cleansing and forgiveness of sin, but it also provided the power to overcome sin. First John 5:4 declares, "For whatever is born of God overcomes the world. And this is the victory that has overcome the world— our faith." Our faith must be stretched and expanded in order to actualize the total victory of the cross.

In First Corinthians 13:11 Paul wrote, "When I was a child, I spoke as a child, I understood as a child, I thought as a child; but when I became a man, I put away childish things." God wants the Church to put away childish things now. Maturity affects everything about the Church. Verses 9 and 10 of First Corinthians 13 read, "For we know in part and we prophesy in part. But when that which is perfect has come, then that which is in part will be done away." Until now, we have known only part, but it is time to walk in the fullness of the blessing of God. This fullness will only be given to the mature—those who have experienced this sanctifying work of the Holy Spirit in their lives.

According to Hebrews 5:8, Jesus was made perfect by the things He suffered, even though He was the Son of God. Jesus was born without sin; He was the spotless Lamb of God. When this verse says He became perfect, it doesn't mean He had to overcome personal flaws. The word *perfect* here means to become everything the Father intends. Jesus could not become all that the Father had purposed until He had fully surrendered His will. We have a purpose in God and are accountable for it. Until we understand this, we will never be what God wants us to be. In the past, because of the immaturity of the Church, our major concern has been who or what we are in relationship to others. We've continually compared ourselves to others. Only when we focus our eyes on the Father can we become like Him. First Corinthians 13:12 says, "For now we see in a mirror, dimly, but then face to face. Now I know in part, but then I shall know just as I also am known." In order for this change to happen, we must refrain from childish ways.

In First John 2:12-14, three levels of Christian maturity are implied: John wrote to the little children, the young men, and the fathers. These three stages of our Christian development are also three dimensions of experience. Today, God is calling the Church to the third level or dimension. Mark 4:28 also refers to three stages of development with the example of grain: first there is a blade, then the head, and finally the full grain in the head. Each stage represents a new dimension of surrender, as well as a new dimension of glory.

The First Stage: Children

Sibling rivalry is often a common problem with young children. Whenever one child gets to do something, the others want to do it too. Children often whine, "But it's not fair!" Yet if each child were treated the same, their growth and potential would be severely limited. Each child requires individual attention according to age, gifting, personality, etc. If we allow their childish demands to influence our decisions, we are not fulfilling our responsibility and proper role as parents. Neither does our heavenly Father allow our immature demands to circumvent His purposes for our lives even though we, like children, constantly concern ourselves with what others are doing.

In John 21, after the resurrection, Jesus appeared to the disciples and asked Peter, "Do you love Me more than these?" Peter firmly replied, "Yes, Lord; You know that I love You." Jesus repeated the same question two more times. Peter became upset, but Jesus was stressing Peter's responsibility to tend and feed His sheep. Jesus continued, "Most assuredly, I say to you, when you were younger, you girded yourself and walked where you wished; but when you are old, you will stretch out your hands, and another will gird you and carry you where you do not wish" (Jn. 21:18). Jesus spoke this to Peter, signifying by what death he would glorify God.

Peter's first response was, "Lord, what about John?" He knew that Jesus loved John, and probably felt some competition from him. Jesus then asked Peter, "If I will that he remain till I come, what is that to you? You follow Me" (Jn. 21:22). This Scripture should come to mind any time we begin to compare ourselves to others in the Church. What does God's plan for me have to do with what He has for someone else? God has a unique way for each of us to glorify His name. A sure sign of immaturity is the tendancy to compare ourselves to others, grumbling to God that no one else has it as hard as we do.

A Personal Example

I clearly recollect when the Lord dealt with my heart in this area. In 1988, I was 34 years old and diagnosed as having muscular dystrophy. I experienced tremendous pain and physical problems. The disease progressed rapidly and had already begun to debilitate me. I have never been very strong physically and sports have never interested me. As a child, I was always the last one chosen for a team. I really couldn't blame the other kids for doing that—I didn't want to be on my team either. I knew I wasn't strong. But now with this disease, the little strength I had began to deteriorate. Even a simple task like holding my baby daughter left me feeling weak and shaky. Walking had always been very relaxing for me, yet now it left me extremely tired and in pain. I began experiencing severe muscle cramps and a constant twitching that absolutely drove me crazy. Every medical report confirmed a progressive deterioration of muscle tissue.

It wasn't long before this condition started affecting me spiritually and emotionally. One day the Lord brought to my mind the Scripture about Peter's life when the Lord said to him that when he was old, another would gird him and take him where he would not want to go. I began to question God, "Why are You allowing this to happen to me?" After all, I had always been faithful to Him. Why wasn't He returning the favor?

I rehearsed every kind of teaching I had heard through the years: I exercised faith, claimed healing, rebuked the disease, and prayed and fasted, but nothing worked. Then the Lord started showing me my heart. Just like Peter and the other disciples who had first responded to Jesus, I was only seeking what God could do for me. God clearly let me know that I could not be in control; *He* was sovereign. We will continually become discouraged and angry with God when we compare our walk to someone else's.

The Lord impressed me to hold two services at Mt. Zion Temple to maintain the momentum of growth we were experiencing. I had some real complaints about doing this and began sharing them with the Lord. In my physical condition, I just knew I couldn't handle two morning services and an evening service each week.

Sundays were already difficult enough for me. While under the anointing, I hardly noticed the pain. However, when I went home following the service, I took medication and continually used a hot tub to try to ease the pain. Often my wife, Bonnie, would massage my muscles so I could attend the evening service. God could have at least made it a little easier for me by speeding up the progress of the new church construction, but it just wasn't His time. I wondered why God would allow all of these things to happen to me when all I ever wanted to do was please Him.

Then I had an intense personal experience with God that changed my perspective and my attitude. By revelation I knew that I had been created for His pleasure (see Rev. 4:11 KJV). The Lord asked me, "Are you going to do what I say?" It was then that I totally surrendered my life to God. Never until that moment had I surrendered everything to the Lord. I told the Lord that whatever He asked me to do, I would do. This was my garden of Gethsemane. Although I hated what was happening to me, I was able to pray, "Father, not my will, but Your will be done." Jesus was tormented by what was happening to Him. He prayed, "O My Father, if it is possible, let this cup pass from Me; nevertheless, not as I will, but as You will" (Mt. 26:39). Hebrews 5:8-9 says, "Though He was a Son, yet He learned obedience by the things which He suffered. And having been perfected, He became the author of eternal salvation, to all who obey Him." We will not be made complete until we totally surrender our will to God. Only then will our lives be salvation or help to others.

At the beginning of my ministry, the Lord spoke an important truth to me about the power of resurrection from the dead. The early Church operated in this realm of power. They were not afraid to face any sickness or problem. They had seen firsthand the power that conquered death. Even Abraham knew the power of resurrection. He and Sarah experienced resurrection life by conceiving and bringing forth a baby in their old age. When Abraham was asked to offer his only son as a sacrifice, he was able to respond to God's command because he believed He would raise him from the dead. The child was conceived and born out of a dead womb, so Abraham believed death had no power over him.

I sought resurrection, but had not realized that before resurrection, there is death. We must be able to face the death of our wills if we are ever to see the power of resurrection. Then I surrendered to God and made the commitment to walk the path He has chosen for me.

As time passed, I felt God was going to heal me. In February of 1988, I had started planning our annual winter vacation to Florida. I always looked forward to this time together with my family, but because of my health, I dreaded going. All I could envision was standing in long lines at Disney World with kids hanging on my arms crying for me to hold them. My arms were so sore and tender that I could hardly tolerate anyone even touching them.

The week before we had planned to leave on vacation, I was at church praying. I had asked the Lord for a special favor. Several times, while praying in tongues, I had prophesied in Spanish and some bilingual members of the congregation understood what I had said. I asked God to allow me to pray in Spanish, announcing my own healing, and to let someone in the church hear and understand so they could tell me. I knew this would confirm my faith and give me strength to face the days ahead.

Just a few minutes after I had prayed, a founding member of our church, Sister Calcote, came in and said that God was going to confirm my healing. I told her what I had prayed. She felt that God said it would be confirmed by the doctors. At this point, it didn't matter to me who would confirm it, as long as it was confirmed.

The day we were to leave for Florida, Sister Calcote came to the church and asked if she could pray for me. We invited Brother Ramirez to join us. Sister Calcote prayed in tongues and Brother Ramirez understood the word God had spoken, but because of his limited ability to speak English, he could not tell us. He shared the word with his family, and they later informed me that God had said, "From this day forward, you will notice a distinct difference in your condition."

When we arrived in Florida, I noticed a tremendous difference in my condition. I remember saying to Bonnie that I couldn't believe how good I felt even though I walked everywhere, stood in long lines, held my children, and even carried my daughter on my shoulders. It wasn't until I returned home from vacation that I learned what had really happened.

I almost canceled my appointment for further testing at Henry Ford Hospital in Detroit because I felt so good. Then I remembered what Sister Calcote had said about the doctors confirming my healing, so I went ahead with the tests. When the doctors began to discuss their findings with me, I knew God's word was being fulfilled. They told me that the results of the biopsy indicated that there was scar tissue in the muscle and the EMG test showed normal.

I had been examined several times before with the EMG test. It was this test that first revealed my disease and it had always indicated abnormal. I asked the doctors how this could be, considering the previous tests. They couldn't explain it, but affirmed that my condition appeared better. When they apologized because they thought I was still experiencing pain, I told them I was free of pain and that God had healed me. I'm not sure if they concurred, but I knew they were relieved to know their results were correct. The doctors confirmed my healing.

The most profound aspect of my healing was the timing. I had totally submitted to God and His purpose for me, which included having two services on Sunday morning. The first Sunday morning that I preached two services was the first Sunday, since I had been in the ministry, that I had preached without pain. My surrender to His will brought the power of resurrection life. I had not just surrendered the service schedule, I had surrendered to God's sovereign will for my life and trusted in His grace to sustain me.

Signs of Immaturity

I have been blessed to see God's grace continually poured out on our church, but I confess that many times when I would see what God was doing in other places, I would wonder why He wasn't doing the same at Mt. Zion Temple. This was the sin of Cain. When he focused on the work of his brother rather than on his own, a spirit of covetousness possessed him. He felt his biggest problem was his brother—and the result was murder. This is the reason Jesus quoted, "I desire mercy and not sacrifice" (Mt. 9:13). As long as we are giving God personal sacrifices, we will compare them to our brothers'. That will alway result in death.

Psalm 33:15 says, "He fashions their hearts individually; He considers all their works." As ministers of the Lord, we should compare ourselves only to Jesus Christ. Only when we look to Him can we clearly see that what the Father required of Him, as well as what He requires of us. We must be totally obedient to Him in everything that He asks of us. But, if God does not ask something, He doesn't want you to offer it. When Samuel judged Saul's disobedience by taking away his right to the kingdom, he said, "Has the Lord as great delight in burnt offerings and sacrifices, as in obeying the voice of the Lord? Behold, to obey is better than sacrifice, and to heed than the fat of rams" (1 Sam. 15:22). Sometimes we are more willing to make sacrifices and give offerings than we are to obey and heed the Lord because our eyes are on men, not God. We must ask ourselves daily, "What does God require of me?"

It would be wonderful if every member of the Body of Christ truly felt the liberty to be what God has called them to be. First Corinthians 12 informs us that God has given diversities of gifts; and with these gifts come different administrations. God has also given a different calling to each of us. The Church consists of a diverse group of people. When we each fulfill our own purpose, we become an effective expression of the Body of Christ. However, if we concentrate on what others are doing and allow the spirit of covetousness entrance, it destroys the power of the unified body.

Paul addressed the Corinthian church, a people full of division and turmoil. He likened them to a human body whose parts had decided that they did not want to continue operating in their God-given purpose because they felt their functions were not as important as another's. When the hand saw the function of the eye it said, in effect, "The body has no need of me." Or the foot, when it saw the greater function of the hand, said, "The body has no need of me." (See First Corinthians 12.)

If we would each realize that we contribute to a purpose greater than our individual function, we would operate in our purpose without envying the function performed by someone else. We must realize that our part or function is vitally important to the whole. Each part must perform its function because no other part can perform it.

Another sign of immaturity is the desire to conform. Conformity is very evident in teenagers, but we all do it to some degree. Many churches promote this behavior by setting standards for everyone to conform to. People compare each other to the standard: "Are they one of us or not?" Although this is evident in the

Church today, God does not want us to be conformed to any religious pattern. He wants a transformed Church. Throughout Church history, as God moved, He challenged the established Church to see if it would be willing to accept people who were different.

A more recent example is the Pentecostal churches needing to accept the Charismatics that God sent into their midst. The Pentecostal churches that received Charismatics have experienced great revival and growth; those who rejected them have become stagnant. As God begins a new work in the Church, we must be willing to walk in a level of Spirit that allows us to accept all transformed believers, whether or not they conform to our standards.

Traditions As Roadblocks

When I graduated from Minister's Candidate School, God spoke a tremendous word to me through the prophetic laying on of hands. He said that a great ministry would come, like that of Elisha, where God would give a ministry of a double portion. God told me that He was going to raise Mt. Zion Temple as a voice during a great visitation He was sending to the earth. One day I asked God when was He going to send the great move of the Spirit that He had promised. From the beginning I have always experienced exceptional blessings from God, but I knew God meant an increase beyond what we had experienced or imagined. God then spoke, "When you can say whoever will, let him come, that is when the fountain of the Lord will really flow in your midst." I was reminded of the great river of life that John saw proceeding from the throne of grace and the call that he heard go forth. Whoever desires, let him come to the river of life (see Rev. 22:17). I knew in my spirit that before we would see the blessing of God in our midst, we had to change.

Without realizing it, like most churches, I had preached a gospel of conformation. When people came to drink of the fountain of life, I set very specific standards for them to follow. Actually, they were roadblocks. I invited people to come to Jesus, but held them back with my rules. God said that He wanted the river to flow and that I must open the way for people to get to it.

Harvest can only come when we break down hindrances and prejudice. The organized church must remain free of religious pride and tradition to maintain the heart of a harvester. Amos prophesied, " 'On that day I will raise up the tabernacle of David, which has fallen down...that they may possess the remnant of Edom, and all the Gentiles who are called by My name' ..." (Amos 9:11-12). It will produce such a harvest that the plowman will overtake the reaper, and the treader of grapes, him who sows the seed. "...The mountains shall drip with sweet wine, and all the hills shall flow with it" (Amos 9:13).

We cannot be a part of the outflow of new wine if we do not pay attention to this important truth. The wine of God will be cut off in our midst if we attempt to confine it by the traditions of men. The Church must be open to all people and set the agenda for racial and cultural harmony. As we flow together as one in the Spirit, we will see people transformed from servants of God to sons of God in the earth.

Submitting to the Father

A person is not transformed by submitting to the ordinances of men, but by a personal encounter with the living God. The most important part of our spiritual walk is to submit ourselves, in complete obedience, to the Father. This is not easy. Hebrews 5:8-9 says that Jesus "learned obedience by the things which He suffered. And having been perfected, He became the author of eternal salvation to all who obey Him." The purpose of the local church is to bring believers to the Father, that His work can be completed in them. They may experience correction, but ultimately they will know fruitfulness and enter a place of relationship with God. When the Church looks to the Father to do the work of sanctification, children will be transformed into sons. If the Church tries to take the place of the Father, she will be like Jezebel and produce bastards—not sons.

It was Jesus' obedience and surrender to God in the garden of Gethsemane that appropriated the power of resurrection life. Hebrews 5:7 says, "...He had offered up prayers and supplications, with vehement cries and tears to Him who was able to save Him from death...." Jesus agonized over not just the pain, but also why He had to die. He had passions like ours. He hadn't done anything wrong. Why must He accept the cross?

Although Jesus cried bitter tears, the Father heard Him because of His godly fear. He surrendered and the

Father imparted enabling grace that was sufficient to allow Him to yield to the cross. When we surrender our wills, we receive God's empowerment. This is why Jesus said in Matthew 16:25, "For whoever desires to save his life will lose it, but whoever loses his life for My sake will find it." We must pick up our crosses and follow God to find life.

The most important thing in life is to surrender and submit to the Father's will. Our perfection comes only by totally yielding to the purpose ordained for us before the foundation of the world. It is our responsibility to walk in that purpose; it is ours alone to perform. It doesn't matter what others do; it matters what you do. It doesn't matter what you think or how you feel about your circumstances. What matters is that you love and trust Jesus. Just as Jesus asked Peter, "Do you love Me?" and Peter replied, "Yes," His ultimate concern was the sheep (see Jn. 21). When we are totally committed to God's purpose, our primary concern will be to feed His sheep. Jesus told Peter, "...when you were younger, you girded yourself and walked where you wished; but when you are old, you will stretch out your hands, and another will gird you and carry you where you do not wish" (Jn. 21:18).

The Second Stage: Young Men

John wrote to the young men because they had overcome the wicked one (see 1 John 2:12-14). The wicked one is he who sits on the throne declaring himself to be God in the holy temple. The holy temple is our body, the place of God's habitation (see 1 Cor. 6:19). God desires to live and rule in us. When we surrender to God, then we can be all that He wants us to be. The Church struggles for its identity. Once we have resolved who we are and what our purpose is, then we can face any adversity in our calling with the resolve to fulfill God's will. Then we will bring glory to the Father.

The Third Stage: Fathers

Finally, John wrote to the fathers because "they have known Him who is from the beginning" (1 John 2:13). As we grow and have children of our own, our perception of our own fathers change. The emphasis switches from our role in pleasing or doing what our fathers expect to that of relationship. It is the same with God. As we mature, we see Him from a different perspective.

In this highest and most intimate level of relationship, we can work as a full-heir son, not a servant. We truly become co-laborers together with God (see 1 Cor. 3:9).

Chapter 7

The Bride's House

Before the Church can bring to birth the sons of God in the earth, we need a greater understanding of the Church's importance in the plan of God. The Father desires to bring forth mature sons. He has created the church family for the purpose of bringing forth children and raising them to maturity. This family, according to the Ephesian letter, is named after the Father of our Lord Jesus Christ and encompasses people both in Heaven and in earth (see Eph. 3:14-15). This family is eternal and is blessed of the Father. It is the Church, called Mt. Zion in the book of Hebrews and the New Jerusalem in Galatians. The Church is the mother of us all.

The concept of the Church is a great paradox. Individually, we become sons of God when we are born again. Collectively, however, we are the Bride of Christ, a mystical spiritual body comprised of believers from every denomination and nation and who have been truly washed in the blood of the Lamb. As the manifold wisdom of God is revealed in the earth, we will learn that we are actually more than both. Our understanding of the whole counsel of God is necessary for our spiritual development. Our individual goal is to obtain full sonship, but before we can do that, we must first understand the place of the mother in the family of God.

The Church: A Feminine Role

A family is not complete without a mother. With the rise of feminism in our society, many people are trying to impose a feminine God on us. They neither see nor understand that the mother, the Church, fulfills this role. They believe traditional Christianity is too paternalistic and allows no place of authority for women. Obviously, they do not understand the plan of the Father. According to Genesis 2:18, God Himself looked at Adam and said, "It is not good that man should be alone; I will make him a helper comparable to him." Ephesians 5:25 tells us that the relationship between husband and wife is the same relationship that Christ has with the Church. God made woman from man. She was a gift to him, yet she was taken from him. God has done the same thing with Christ and the Church. He is presenting a Bride to Himself. The Church is this Bride, taken from His own side. She will not only be a wife to her Espoused; she also will assume the role of mother in the earth.

There has been much controversy, especially in mainline churches, over a woman's place in the church. Thus they have created a more feminine expression of God. Although they are well-meaning in their desire to improve the status of women, their view has been distorted by the liberal feminism that is opposed to the structure of the God-ordained family. Some have changed the words of hymnals and prayers to downplay the masculine character (Fatherhood) of God. In some cases, they have inserted references to a female or unisex God, even though God is revealing Himself, like never before, as the Father. Dreadful are the devil's devices to destroy the work of God in the earth. In John 5:19 Jesus said, "...the Son can do nothing of Himself, but what He sees the Father do...." This is the reason the enemy seeks to eliminate or distort our perception of the Father. Without His chastening in the house, we will grow up as bastards and not sons.

Statistics about the problems arising from homes without fathers should testify to the need for a father. With the breakdown of the family structure, many inner city families have become poverty-stricken. The deterioration of the father figure is a major problem our nation must deal with before our cities can be restored. The father's role is also essential for a strong Church. The Church is God's feminine expression on the earth, but He is still the Father of the house.

The father's role does not negate the influence of a mother, nor the fact that God does have a maternal concern for His people. When Jesus came into Jerusalem just before His crucifixion, He said, "O

Jerusalem, Jerusalem...! How often I wanted to gather your children together, as a hen gathers her chicks under her wings, but you were not willing!" (Mt. 23:37) The Father wants His people to experience the nurturing care that only a mother can give. He shares this responsibility with the Bride. The Bride is to birth His children and care for them in the earth (see Heb. 10:20). When we examine the role of the mother in a family, we can better understand God's desire for His Church and then fulfill our proper role, not usurping the Father's.

The Importance of Function

Knowing our proper role or function is very important. In the beginning, God brought all the animals before Adam to be named. It would appear that Adam did not give them just any name, but identified each by function. The Bible says that after he had named them, he did not find a helper suitable to him (see Gen. 2:20). Adam discovered a role or function that had not been filled, so God filled it. We see this identification again when Adam named Eve. He identified her by function; she was the mother of all living (see Gen. 3:20). Then man took his proper place of authority and fulfilled his purpose by taking dominion over creation. Thus with every part functioning in its proper place, creation was complete.

Ephesians 3:9-11 recounts the purpose of the mystery that was in the mind and heart of God from the beginning. Mankind was created in the image and likeness of God. Just as Eve was created from Adam, so was man created from God Himself. No other creation could properly function in this role.

On the Day of Pentecost, Jesus poured His Spirit into His Bride. When we receive the Holy Spirit, we receive God. As God ultimately purposed, the Church can now function in what only God could perform. The gifts of the Holy Spirit are diverse, placed in man to enable him to perform functions of God. The Church must understand that there are certain things God will not do for us because He has appointed them to us. The Church has great power and can offer solutions to the world, but instead often sits idly by, waiting for God to do something. The great move of God in this day will be through the Church. We, like the Ephesian church, need revelation to have the eyes of our understanding enlightened, to know the hope of His calling and the riches of the glory of His inheritance in the saints (see Eph. 1:18).

An optimal marital arrangement is when two people, with different gifts and resources, function together as one. Each supplies what the other lacks. Likewise, in His relationship with us, God has indeed decided to limit Himself. When we realize that God has ordained certain functions for us (the Church), we can begin to understand the greatness of the glory that He has bestowed on us. John received this revelation on the Isle of Patmos, when he saw the Bride who walked in the glory of her Husband. An angel said to him, "Come, I will show you the bride, the Lamb's wife" (Rev. 21:9). He then carried John in the Spirit to a great and high mountain, showing him the great city, the holy Jerusalem, descending out of Heaven from God. John

goes on to describe that her light was like a most precious stone, speaking of great beauty and splendor.
(See Revelation 21:10-11.) Oh, what glory the Father
wants to bestow upon the Bride!

A Bride Adorned

I believe the most significant part of John's revelation is how the Bride prepares herself for her Husband.
The marriage supper of the Lamb will not take place
until the Bride has made herself ready (arrayed herself
in "fine linen, clean and bright, for the fine linen is the
righteous acts of the saints" [Rev. 19:8]). It is time for
the Church to make herself ready, to agree with the
Spirit's call to come to the marriage supper of the
Lamb.

The marriage supper does not necessarily take
place at the end of time. When you study the Scripture
closely, you will see that the menu is definitely not one
you would select for a wedding. According to Revelation 19:18, the menu includes the flesh of kings, the
flesh of captains, the flesh of mighty men, the flesh of
horses, etc. Our spiritual eyes must be opened to the
significance of this chapter. It does not refer to a literal
meal, but to a time when God will deliver all the
enemies of the Bride to her on a silver platter.

We see a type of this with the wicked ruler, Herod,
during the time of Christ. For Herod's birthday, the
daughter of his wife Herodias danced before him. He
was so impressed with her that he promised to give her
whatever she would ask. Her mother urged her to request the head of John the Baptist. Even though her

request was evil, the king was duty-bound to fulfill his promise. (See Mark 6.) This may not be a comfortable comparison, but the fact remains that when the Church fulfills her function to please her Husband, the Father is bound by His promise to avenge her of all her enemies.

When Isaiah prophesied about the desolate woman who becomes blessed of God, it refers to the Gentile church (see Is. 54). God promises to remove her reproach, adorn her with colorful gems, instruct her children, and establish a wall of protection around her. God continues to say that "No weapon formed against you shall prosper, and every tongue which rises against you in judgment you shall condemn. This is the heritage of the servants of the Lord, and their righteousness is from Me..." (Is. 54:17).

Over the past few years, the Church has been under intense scrutiny by the secular media. The result has been many embarrassing revelations and what seems to be unfair criticism. Thus, Christians have lashed out in defense. This behavior is so unladylike. This is not a well-received statement in our feminist-oriented society, but our Husband wants to be our protector. Our Husband would prefer that we spend our time adorning ourselves to please Him and leave the fighting to Him. We need to learn to exercise discretion, retreat from our instinctive nature to fight, and become what the Husband desires—a pure and chaste Bride.

In First Peter 3:3, the apostle Peter addresses the issue of women's adornment. He instructs the wives not to focus on their outward beauty: adorning or arranging the hair, wearing gold, or putting on fine apparel. The adornment of the true bride should be the hidden person of the heart with the incorruptible ornament of a gentle and quiet spirit, which is very precious in the sight of God. He continues to say that the women of old also adorned themselves in this manner, being submissive to their own husbands.

For years the organized Church has tried to impress God with her outward appearance while God was concerned about her heart. The Bride needs to learn how to please her Espoused. An admonition given by the prophet Zephaniah warned those settled in complacency that the day of the Lord would be a day of trouble and distress, of devastation and desolation (see Zeph. 1:15). Why? Jerusalem would want God's blessing, but would not accept the responsibility to seek after righteousness and humility. Today we long for the Bridegroom to come, yet don't realize He wants us to prepare. The Bride must be sensitive and responsive to the desires of her Husband.

The emphasis changed from inward to outward adornment because changing the outward is easier. Religions that strictly follow dress standards believe they are choosing the harder way, the most sacrificial way. They pride themselves on how holy and righteous they appear. Jesus, during His earthly ministry, addressed this issue. He told the scribes and Pharisees, "...you cleanse the outside of the cup and dish, but inside they are full of extortion and self-indulgence" (Mt. 23:25). He said, "...first cleanse the inside of the cup and dish, that the outside of them may be clean also" (Mt. 23:26). They never understood His teachings because they honored God with their lips, not with their hearts (see Mt. 15:8). Our love for God must not be an outward show or form because He desires a people who love Him with all of their hearts. The makeup of our human hearts is really no different from God's; He also desires love. The Bible declares that God is love (see 1 John 4:8). Because love is His substance, it is a vital part of our relationship with Him.

Not Our Own

The Scripture tells us that in the marriage union, our bodies are not our own; they belong to our spouse (see 1 Cor. 7:4). After we have given our hearts to God, then and only then does He want our bodies, our entire beings. We are not our own. We willingly surrender ourselves to Him for His pleasure.

When I suffered with muscular dystrophy, that very painful and debilitating disease, I began to complain to God: "I deserve better than this. How could You allow this to happen when I've been so faithful to You?" As I was lying before the Lord feeling sorry for myself, God spoke, "For My pleasure were you created" (see Rev. 4:11 KJV). This word astounded and shocked me! All of my life I had asked the Lord to use me and now, when I was being used, I was complaining about it. A danger to any relationship is when one of the partners feels used. Once bitterness springs up, the relationship is usually destroyed. With the enemy's influence, I was allowing this very thing to happen in my relationship

107

with God. All at once, an intense desire to please the Lord came over me. At that moment, I cried out, "If I'm to serve You in constant pain, or from a wheelchair, or even die prematurely, all I know is that for Your pleasure was I created!"

It's hard for me to express what happened that day. I was almost too embarrassed to share it with anyone. The only way I can describe it is to say it was like the intimate union of a husband and wife, where their only desire is to bring pleasure to the other. I kept this experience to myself until I found a Scripture to confirm it. Psalm 37:4 says, "Delight yourself also in the Lord, and He shall give you the desires of your heart."

The word *delight* in Hebrew means to be soft, pliable, and figuratively effeminate. In one place it is translated to mean sporting oneself, and in another, as delicate, as in describing women who are comely or tender. This type of experience with God transformed the way I served Him. I could now serve the Lord with gladness of heart and with an intimacy I had never before experienced.

A Secret Relationship

God wants an intimate relationship with us—a secretive relationship. In marriage, a man and a woman become one flesh. According to the Scriptures, this type of intimacy should be reserved for the marriage relationship. Although there were times in the Scriptures where men had more than one wife at one time, this was never God's perfect will. He ordained this intimacy to be with only one person for a lifetime.

Marriage partners share something that they never share with any other person. This is true intimacy—a special secrecy between a husband and wife. When this occurs, the bond of marriage is sealed with a oneness that ultimately enhances the covenant between them. Intimacy seals the words of the marriage covenant, unlike any other contract a person may enter during his lifetime.

God wants a relationship with the Bride just like the one I've described. When the outwardly pious, religious people of Jesus' day marched through the streets, He showed scorn for them. He said that they appeared holy, but they had their reward—the admiration of people (see Mt. 6:2,5). God, on the other hand, is looking for people to please Him instead of men. That is why our public piety is not acceptable to God. The strength of our walk comes from our private relationship with Him.

He wants us to pray and give our alms privately so He can reward us openly (see Mt. 6:3-4,6). When we secretly do something for God, our relationship with Him becomes more intimate. He then returns His love in a way that will make others notice. As I yielded to God, He said that He would receive me into everlasting habitations. I understood what He meant; God was talking about my intimate relationship with Him and my willingness to love and receive people who may never benefit me or Mt. Zion Temple.

The power and glory of God will be demonstrated through those who have unselfishly and discreetly committed their lives to Him. My satisfaction is in knowing that I am fulfilling His desires because I was created for His pleasure.

Chapter 8

The Mother's House

Just as Eve was chosen to be the mother of all living, so the Bride of Christ has been chosen to be the mother who will bring forth the family of God. In the New Testament, she was intended to bring forth all of God's children. Some of the most significant people mentioned in the Bible were barren women whose greatest desire was to conceive and bear children. Their example was given to us to emphasize the position of the mother in the family of God.

We live in a generation that has been remarkably successful in altering and belittling a mother's role. Fortunately, this is proving to be a decreasing trend. The news media commonly reports that a current baby boom is resulting from a generation of older women having children. Many women who thought they would be fulfilled with careers or other pursuits are discovering that their instinctive desire to birth and nurture children has been severely neglected. They have found that life without a family of their own is unfulfilled and dissatisfying.

The Satisfaction of Seed

Jesus commanded His disciples to go into all the world and preach the gospel (see Mk. 16:15). This is known as the great commission of the Church. The Church, the Bride, must also understand how wonderful and powerful it is to experience procreation with God. Isaiah 53 reveals that as Jesus agonized on the cross, enduring intense suffering and shame, He saw His seed and was satisfied. Most women will confess that the painful memory of childbirth begins to fade the moment that precious newborn is placed in their arms. The joy and pleasure a new baby brings is not to be compared to the pain. We need to receive the Father's seed, the anointed word of God, and make a sacrificial commitment to bear the pain and responsibility of pregnancy, birth, and child-rearing, to bring forth children in the Father's house. When we present spiritual children to our beloved Husband and focus on the joy it brings to us, the pain and responsibility seem small in comparison.

> *"Sing, O barren, you who have not borne! Break forth into singing, and cry aloud, you who have not labored with child! For more are the children of the desolate than the children of the married woman," says the Lord* (Isaiah 54:1).

112

Throughout the Scriptures, God used barren women to bring forth His elect. For example, Sarah brought forth Isaac, Rachel brought forth Joseph and Benjamin, Hannah brought forth Samuel, and Elizabeth brought forth John the Baptist. There are many stories in the Bible where women needed divine intervention to bring forth the seed of promise. By studying the examples of their faith in seemingly impossible circumstances, we can better understand how necessary it is for us to move into a greater dimension of faith. The Church may appear to be barren and may experience many difficulties and impurities, but as we walk in a new dimension of faith, we will see the greatest harvest of our time!

Also recorded in these stories is the anguish and distress that these barren women experienced because they could not conceive. Since the Bible is God's Word for today and reveals His desire for us, we should not relegate this burden to the women of old. Our present society has downplayed the importance of childbearing and has replaced it with a fear of overpopulation. We cannot let modern philosophy replace the true burden of our heavenly Father for more sons. After Jesus suffered, He saw His seed, which prolonged His days, and His soul was satisfied (see Is. 53:10-11). God wants children. The purpose of His intimacy with the Church is for her to bring forth children. God desires to propagate Himself in the earth. Christ, the Husband of the Church, awaits replication of Himself in His children. It is God's desire to have many sons in the earth.

Jesus revealed the Father's heart in the parable of the great supper (Lk. 14:15-24). The master had prepared a feast, inviting many people, but each had an excuse for not coming. The master told his servant to go quickly into the highways and hedges, and compel them to come in. He was not satisfied until his house was full. A full house, however, is just the beginning of God's expectations. The children must then be brought to maturity.

The Church's Role as a Mother

Proverbs 31:10-31 describes a virtuous wife. Her worth is far above rubies; the heart of her husband trusts her; she does her husband good and not evil. Her role also includes three important functions: she assumes the responsibilities of providing for her children, she extends her hands to the poor, and she seeks to make her husband known in the gates. This is a true demonstration of God's desire for the Church to be a place to nurture the spiritual children in the family; nevertheless, this is not enough. The Father has commissioned us to be the salt of the earth also (see Mt. 5:13). Thus the Church should be a place of equipping the saints for the work of ministry (see Eph. 4:12).

Protective Care

First, the Church must assume responsibility for providing and caring for her children. After my first child, Loren, was born, I remember having such a fear that something bad might happen to him. All at once I became aware that Bonnie and I were ultimately responsible for his safety and welfare. I was over-whelmed by the potential dangers in our house, like poisonous cleaning supplies, glass objects, stairways, etc. Keeping him safe was my only concern. I put gates across the stairways, protective stops on all the cup-board doors, and then placed all the breakables out of reach. I particularly remember reading one day that a major cause of death among small children was drown-ing in the toilet. I constantly reminded Bonnie to close the bathroom door or make sure the lid was down. Al-though this may seem humorous, my paranoia was a result of my deep concern for my child's safety.

While I was in prayer, the Lord spoke to my spirit, "We need to childproof the house." The Church must take her place as a mother in the house. Our main con-cern must be to ensure the safety and welfare of the children of God and to nurture them until they've reached maturity. The house of God must be a place of safety, a protected environment where the children of God can grow to maturity. There will be a great harvest in the days ahead, but the Father will not send His children to a house that has not been childproofed.

Isaiah prophesied, "There shall come forth a Rod from the stem of Jesse" (Is. 11:1a). This Rod speaks of authority. According to the Scriptures, when this Rod branches out, the earth shall be full of the knowledge of the Lord, the nursing child will play by the cobra's hole; the weaned child shall put his hand in the viper's den; a little child shall lead them; the cow and the bear shall graze and their young ones shall lie down together, for they shall not hurt nor destroy in God's holy mountain (see Is. 11:6-9). This does not speak of a future millennia, but of God's desire for the Church today. The Father is the defender of the house, but the mother is the protector of the house. My primary concern as a pastor is the safety of the Church's children. They must be allowed a place where they can learn, grow, and even fail. The house must provide an atmosphere of encouragement and love. Anything potentially dangerous should be removed and a guard must be raised against any intruder that might harm the children. When Isaiah's vision comes to pass, the children will be able to grow up in a peaceful and safe environment.

Interpretation

A good mother understands the maturing process of her children and realizes her joint responsibility with the Father to train and discipline them. In the Church, confusion arises when no one knows whose responsibility it is to train the children. Is it God's responsibility or is it the responsibility of the Church? Proverbs 1:8 states, "My son, hear the instruction of your father, and do not forsake the law of your mother." The management structure of the family and the Church is defined here. The word *law* is originally translated as Torah, or the interpretation of the written law.

When God gave Moses instruction for His people, Moses interpreted and gave an application of the law to them. Later it became known as the law of Moses. Moses simplified the law so the people could understand and relate to it in their daily lives. The law of

God is eternal and unchanging, but particular inter-
pretations and applications of the law have changed
with each generation. Each dispensation requires an
interpretation of God's dealings with His people. As
time and society change, the enactment of God's Word
ultimately changes as well. Church laws change and
people often feel confused because they do not understand the mother's responsibility to interpret the instruction of the Father.

Administration

In a traditional family setting, the father sets the
vision for the home and family while the mother ad-
ministers it, considering the personal needs of each
child and the family. I've learned by counseling couples
that men usually announce the headlines and the
women do the detail work. I know that many times,
when I make a logical decision about the children, my
wife Bonnie may bring something to my attention that
I may have overlooked, such as their emotional or individual needs. The different functions of a father and
a mother can lead to conflict, but if both realize their
differences and work together, they will learn to ap-
preciate their uniqueness and function. When they
work together, they create a wonderfully balanced
home life. Meeting the emotional and personal needs of
others has been delegated to the Church. When we hug
someone with His love, we make Him real to them in a
way they understand. We are His representatives, vessels of His Spirit in human form.

Solomon writes in Proverbs 4:3, "When I was my
father's son, tender and the only one in the sight of my

mother," he amplifies the sensitivity of a child's needs. A mother tenderly nurtures each child according to his individual needs. Bonnie and I have three children: Loren, Billy, and Ashley, who are all unique. As their father, I tend to approach situations in a businesslike manner, treating and expecting the same from each. Often I forget to consider their individual personalities or needs when dealing with them. However, Bonnie looks at situations in a different light.

I remember when our sons Loren and Billy had both outgrown their bicycles. I thought the logical thing to do was to purchase a new bicycle for Loren and give Loren's old one to Billy. Bonnie was not pleased with this idea at all. She felt Billy should have a new bicycle of his own because he always got hand-me-downs. Thinking I had the perfect solution, I offered Billy money to take Loren's old bicycle. He wouldn't even consider my offer. Billy had his heart set on a new bicycle too. Bonnie was right. She then told me she would buy the bicycle with some money she had saved for herself. She didn't think twice about making a sacrifice for her son. She was not interfering or trying to cause discord. She was just fulfilling her role as a mother. Her concern was for her children and she made sure they each received care and attention. When I saw things from her perspective, I could not refuse Billy a new bicycle.

Intercession

It would be wonderful if the Church would truly become a mother of intercession, one whose heart is for her children in administering the love of her Husband. The Lord has called our local church to be a "City of Refuge", a place where the love of God is evident. We are seeing bruised and broken people come to us. Many of them have been wounded in churches that did not fulfill their proper role or operate in love. When the Church tries to duplicate or usurp the role of the Father, people suffer. A home without a father is dysfunctional and the lack severely affects the children, but one without a mother is just as tragic.

A good example of a true intercessor is demonstrated in the life and ministry of Moses. God told Moses that He was going to destroy the children of Israel because of their sin, but that He would make a great nation out of Moses and his seed (see Ex. 32:9-10). Moses interceded on behalf of the children of Israel rather than seize an opportunity for personal greatness. He was willing to give up everything for the people.

Jesus Christ, our greatest example, sacrificed and gave His life for His children. Leaders in the house of God must follow His example. A true leader does not strive for personal gain; instead his life is given to care for the people. Isn't this how a mother treats her children? She wouldn't hesitate to give her life for any one of them. God is looking for local churches to fulfill this role today.

Wouldn't this loving attitude temper the preaching of many sermons? When leaders hear God speak of coming judgment, it is their responsibility to position themselves as intercessors for the people. Unfortunately, many preachers relish words of judgment—it gives them something to preach and makes them feel superior. Likewise, as God judges our great nation, we cannot simply use it as an opportunity to preach. We must be willing to fall on our knees and cry out for mercy. We must be willing to give ourselves as an offering. God wants us to be intercessors. Isaiah 59:16 says, "He saw that there was no man, and wondered that there was no intercessor; therefore His own arm brought salvation for Him; and His own righteousness, it sustained Him."

Jesus fulfilled the role of an intercessor when He came to earth. As the Body of Christ, we also are called to continue this function. If we would line up our attitude with God's, we'd experience a revival like never before. When the world begins to see the Church as a loving, nurturing family instead of a dysfunctional one or one that pronounces judgment and destruction, they will come in like a flood. In Jesus' day, the multitudes followed Him hoping to get their needs met, and it's no different today. It was the religious order of Jesus' day that could not receive Him or His ministry.

Jesus was wholly committed to the people, yet His ministry ended by Him giving His life on the cross. He never allowed people to deter Him; He knew His purpose was to fulfill the will of the Father. Moses, however, was distracted from his call. In an emotional outburst, he struck the rock when God told him to speak to it. He was harsh to the people and called them rebels, saying, "Must I bring water out of this rock for you!" (See Numbers 20:7-11.) Though Moses had good reason to be upset, he should never have displayed this anger before the people. He had fallen from a place of intercession and failed to sanctify God before the people. Therefore, he could not enter the land of promise, his inheritance.

Many sermons today fall under this category. When the preacher speaks very loud and with much emotion, the congregation thinks he is anointed; yet many times he is really manifesting his anger before the people. This is not the conduct of a true intercessor or leader. It is no wonder many Christians never reach the promised blessing of God.

As a prophetically-motivated person, I am concerned about people who claim to be prophets of God when their real motivation seems to stem from a critical nature. The Bible records that Moses was a great prophet, so we must not fail to see his love and commitment to the people. The same holds true for all the prophets of old, as well as in our ultimate example, Jesus Christ. Jesus said, "A new commandment I give to you, that you love one another; as I have loved you, that you also love one another" (Jn. 13:34). Jesus was willing to die for the people and He asks us to deny ourselves, take up our cross, and follow Him (see Mt. 16:24). We need to understand that a true intercessor's heart is always for the people.

Feeding

As a mother, it is also the Church's place to prepare the food. A virtuous woman provides or prepares food

for her household (see Prov. 31:14-15). The father
makes provision for the food, but the mother often
functions as the preparer. We must remember that
man does not live by bread alone, but by every word
that proceeds from the mouth of God (see Mt. 4:4). To
live, we must receive bread from the Father. The
mother must prepare the bread and make it desirable
for the family to eat. The bread may have to be broken
into small pieces for the younger children, those not
mature enough to eat it whole. The older children are
able to eat it, but sometimes may fuss about the taste.
She cannot force them to eat, so she prepares food in a
way that is desirable to them. A wise mother also
knows that she cannot feed her family just what ap-
peals to them—she must prepare a well-balanced diet.
The Church must do the same. We cannot have a one-
doctrine or out-of-balance ministry; otherwise the
children will become malnourished.

Outreach

The virtuous woman extends her hands to the poor
(see Prov. 31:20). Often when we think about women of
the Bible, we picture them only residing behind the
walls of their own homes. The woman in Proverbs 31
lays this myth to rest. She reaches far beyond the
perimeters of her own house. She not only nurtures her
own children, but she reaches out to the children of the
city. Many times the Church has only concerned herself
with the children inside the house. This reflects a
woman who does not have the heart of a true mother,
but one who desires to build only for herself. A true
mother reaches out to any child in need.

The Old Testament clearly reveals the heart of the Father. His concern is not just for His own, but also for the fatherless, the widows, and the poor (see Ps. 68:5-6). The Church must have the heart of God in order to bring glory to Him. If the Church only seeks to bring glory to herself, she has lost the glory of the Father. The Father's house must be one of reaching out to all in need. Outreach will be one of the signs of a church flowing in the blessings of this present move of God. People in the world today are looking for someone to reach out to meet their needs. Someone has to care for the children of this generation. The Father has asked the Bride to reach out to those no one else cares for. The Father's provision should be extended beyond the church walls to the community, to a dying generation. As the Church believes in her Husband's ability to provide, she will see His provision increased.

Reflection

Finally, a virtuous woman's family is a direct reflection of her husband. As the husband provides for the family and takes care of business outside the home, he relies on the mother to care for the family. The woman in Proverbs 31 cares for her home and family, always keeping her husband in mind. She desires to bring him honor and make him known in the gates. Everything she does reflects the honor and love she has toward him.

God says in Isaiah 60:7, "...and I will glorify the house of My glory." He will send His glory to a house that seeks to bring glory to Him. God does not honor building monuments to the glory of men; He only honors those who seek to bring honor to Him. The Church, the mother of the family of God, cannot seek to produce spiritual children for her own glory, in order to make herself look good. She represents her Husband and all the glory goes to Him. When the Church realizes this, God will truly come and place His glory upon her. Just as a virtuous woman brings glory to her husband by bearing him godly seed, so must the Church honor her Husband by presenting Him with godly seed. We need to commit ourselves totally to God and raise His children to the glory of their Father in His house.

Selfless

I have learned that the greatest degree of our maturity occurs when we begin to have children. When the Scriptures say in First Timothy 2:15 that a woman is saved in childbearing, it cannot possibly mean salvation with God, nor can it mean that women must have children to be saved. Instead, it refers to the personal salvation or change she experiences. A common saying is that only God's love is greater than a mother's love. Her concern is no longer for herself, but for her children. In John 15:13, Jesus said of this self-sacrificing love, "Greater love has no one than this, than to lay down one's life for his friends." A mother should not be the only person in the household who experiences this selfless love, even though she is the one most affected because she may have a closer relationship and spend more time with the children.

Many women choose to suppress their mothering instincts. Many self-centered women reject their responsibilities by aborting their babies before they can make demands upon their time, finances, or energy. On the other hand, many women abuse, neglect, and refuse to love or nurture their children. In these instances the result is either a dead or an abused, dysfunctional child. Neither child realizes his full potential. When a mother responds to her God-given instincts and responsibilities, her life is transformed. Like Christ, she learns to love selflessly. The welfare of the children becomes her priority. The Church must take her rightful place as the mother in the family of God.

Chapter 9

A House of Full-Grown Sons

A young child is no different from a servant, even though he is an heir to all that belongs to the Father. He remains under the guidance of tutors and governors until a time appointed by his father. (See Galatians 4:1-2.) It is very important for us to be as little children; otherwise we cannot enter into the Kingdom of God. Also, even though we are heirs or children of God, we need to learn to be servants as well. At the same time, we cannot remain as mere children or even just as servants, for God has called us to full maturity—to sonship.

In Paul's writings to the Corinthian church, he clearly shows that when he wanted to feed them meat, he could only feed them milk (see 1 Cor. 3:1-2). Although he had ministered to them for a long time, he still considered them nursing babies, or immature. The writer to the Hebrews wrote the same thing; when they should have been teachers, they needed someone to teach them (see Heb. 5:12). It is still true of the Church today. Although the cry of the Spirit is to go on to maturity, the cry of the Church is for someone to cater to her every need. (The primary reason for her immaturity is the humanistic structure of the Church.)

The Church Family

There is no easy way to help children mature. However, God did provide a help—the family structure. Raising children to maturity in the Father's house is the responsibility of the family of God. Leaders are to ensure that the family functions properly so the desire of the Father's heart for mature children is fulfilled.

Today we are witnessing great devastation in our nation because of dysfunctional families. The household of God must be guarded so this same devastation does not occur in the Church. Multitudes have been abused and neglected because of dysfunctional church families. The Church must be a place that encourages and allows the development of children.

When we think of the Church as a family, we also need to understand its purpose. We know it is a place of reproduction because God told Adam and Eve, the first family, to multiply and fill the earth. We know that the family is to be a place of nurturing and understanding. Children must be loved and properly cared for by their mother. However, the ultimate goal of the family is to train the children so they will become responsible adults. If children are provided with the proper training and the necessary skills, they will live a productive life. Then, in turn, they will begin the same process of reproduction and nurturing.

As parents, we are reluctant to see our children grow up, but it would be horrible if they didn't. Those cute little things they do as babies are embarrassing when a full-grown adult does them. I don't expect my son, when he is 30 years old, to ask his mother if he should take a shower or brush his teeth. The heavenly Father feels the same way about His children. Those who should be mature adults in the family of God are still babes. The structure of the Church family must be set in order so the Church can produce spiritual children who mature to be the pride and joy of their Father.

A great resurgence to restore the family back to its original biblical pattern is taking place in the Church today. There is a godly principle for every authority structure in the Body of Christ. Although we have lifted up our voices against secular humanist ideas that are destroying the family, we have allowed them to influence the operation of the Church. An individual family unit cannot reach its full potential unless each family member is equipped by the local church to be everything God wants him or her to be. Just as a natural family equips children for life, the Church must also be a place that equips people for service. In order for this to occur, proper authority structures must be in place.

The Father's Role

Because authority in the ministry is based upon relationship, we need to understand and define relationship as it applies to the family structure. The member most responsible for ensuring that the children are raised properly is the father. This in no way discounts the mother's nurturing role, but it is the instruction and chastisement of the father that brings a child to maturity. Hebrews 12:7-8 says, "If you endure chastening, God deals with you as with sons...but if you are without chastening...then you are illegitimate and not sons."

Children must experience the guiding and chastening hand of a father lest they be left as bastards or illegitimate sons. We are living in a time when we will begin to see the Father as never before. Malachi 4 speaks about a time when the hearts of the fathers will be turned to the children and the hearts of the children to the fathers. During this time, fathering ministries will manifest in the Church. People with love and authority will guide the Church family to a new height or maturity in God. There is a tremendous lack of people demonstrating true God-given authority in the world. When the Church learns to demonstrate it, the world will sit up and take notice. The world cries out for true leadership and it's time for the Church to set an example.

The fivefold ministries listed in Ephesians 4:11-15 include apostles, prophets, evangelists, pastors, and teachers. The Scriptures say that these particular ministries are to equip the saints for the work of ministry and edify the Body until it comes to the unity of the faith and knowledge of the Son of God. "That we should no longer be children, tossed to and fro and carried about with every wind of doctrine...but, speaking the truth in love, may grow up in all things..." (Eph. 4:14-15). Our goal must be to become mature people, fully equipped for service in the Kingdom of our Father.

Our heavenly Father reaches out to the Church through the ministry. This issue of the leadership's function is rather sensitive and must be approached very carefully. A proper balance must be maintained between God's direct role with His people and the role of the father through the ministry. Leadership that usurps the place of the heavenly Father will be too authoritative and stifle the growth of the people. On the other hand, leadership without the Father's involvement will be very loving and nurturing, but too passive to lead or direct. David said in Psalm 26:12, "My foot stands in the even place; in the congregations I will bless the Lord." In order to be a blessing to the congregation, leadership must be balanced.

The house of the Lord needs father figures. Paul warned the Corinthian church, "For though you might have ten thousand instructors in Christ, yet you do not have many fathers" (1 Cor. 4:15a). Therefore, he urged them to imitate him. He would be their father figure and therefore assumed a place of authority over them.

The anointing upon his life and the work he accomplished in their midst were credentials enough for ministry; yet he had to develop a father relationship with them before he could assume a place of authority.

True Authority

There is a vast difference between authority and power. Power can be given to us, but authority must be earned. All believers have a measure of power. As Jesus said, we receive power after the Holy Ghost has come upon us (see Acts 1:8 KJV). What we really need to see, though, is authority. There have been many teachings on authority, but we have failed to realize that the lack of authority is not the fault of the children, wives, or congregations. The real problem stems from a lack of true leadership. Many people in leadership want respect based upon their position, but the Bible teaches us that position is gained because of respect. There is a vast difference in these two approaches.

Many people believe that the women's liberation movement originated because some rebellious women wanted authority, but it actually started because men lacked true authority. Often men do not take the initiative to promote change; therefore, women are forced to. Malachi prophesied that revival would begin when the hearts of the fathers were turned to the children; then the hearts of the children would be turned to the fathers (see Mal. 4). People in the Church are crying out for godly leadership.

The lack of true authority is a direct result of the character or heart condition of the leaders. Today the

Lord is correcting this problem by raising up shepherds after His own heart. Jeremiah lamented against the shepherds of his day, "Woe to the shepherds who destroy and scatter the sheep of My pasture!" (Jer. 23:1). God never allows the shortcomings of man to destroy His people. If necessary, He will scatter the sheep and raise up true shepherds in their midst who will feed and care for them. The sheep will no longer fear or lack for they will have strong shepherds who will take care of them.

The Need for Strong Leadership

When God raises up true shepherds, the sheep who recognize the anointing will respect and give these shepherds the honor they deserve. Much of the instability and breakdown of social order results from poor leadership. Since the 1960's social revolution, there has been a total deterioration of respect for all types of authority, law, and order in America. As true leadership fails, a corresponding cycle of rebellious people governed by weak and indecisive leadership is produced. Society tends to blame leadership for all the problems in the world rather than seeing them as prompters of solutions. This trend must be reversed in the Church if we are to ever achieve excellency in the Kingdom of God. When we learn to respect authority and follow leadership, we will advance and take our inheritance—the land of promise. This cannot happen unless true leadership returns to the Church.

Not long ago, the Lord spoke that it was time for the Church to go in and possess the land, that we were a

Joshua generation. I began hearing different aspects of this word from different sources. Knowing that out of the mouths of two or three witnesses every word is established, I knew it was time for a generation to go forth to possess their full inheritance in God. As God raises us up, He will also raise up leaders having the same spirit as Joshua and Caleb. They were chosen of God to lead the people into the Promised Land because they completely trusted and followed the commands of God.

Leaders today want to be excused from their weaknesses in the name of God's grace; however, if the leader's character is compromised, so is the strength of the people. The Word is very specific about the high standards that must be demonstrated by leadership in the Church (i.e., 1 Tim. 3). They not only should be respected and have a good report in the Church, but their lives should demonstrate their integrity even before the world.

On the other hand, the family of God also must learn to respect its leaders. If we do not respect them, the world never will. When God chooses someone for leadership, He begins to magnify him before the people. Joshua is a good example. He was chosen to lead the children of Israel into the Promised Land, but before he actually led them, God performed a miracle by parting the Jordan River. This miracle established Joshua's credibility before the people. As seen throughout Church history, whenever God starts a new work, He not only demonstrates His miraculous power to give credibility to the move, He also promotes the leader in the eyes of the people. The family of God needs to honor them. Otherwise we become vulnerable to the enemy. When we begin to show respect to God's ordained leaders, His power will be renewed in our midst.

The Fear of the Lord

When the children of Israel were preparing to enter into the Promised Land, they were first established in the fear of the Lord. It was during this period of time that the words *dreadful, terrible,* and *awesome* were used to describe God. These are not words one would use today to describe a loving and merciful God, but rather to instill pictures of a God who must be feared.

One of the greatest strategies in warfare is to intimidate the enemy. If you can plant fear in the heart of the enemy, you have the battle half won. My generation is a witness to the success of this tactic. Communist powers have continually threatened to take over the world and they constantly paraded their strength. Each year on May Day, the streets of the Soviet Union were filled with soldiers armed for war and they displayed their latest high-tech military equipment. Their intimidation tactics worked to a great extent. The fear of war motivated the United States to spend trillions of dollars on defense. Many American politicians used the Communist threat as part of their platform to gain votes from a fearful society.

When the Iron Curtain collapsed, we discovered that the system Kruschev declared would replace capitalism, couldn't even feed its own people. It was only a matter of time before the truth prevailed, yet we feared and anticipated a Communist takeover of the world.

Another good example is demonstrated in nature. We do not believe in evolution, but the Word does say that the attributes of the invisible God can be seen in creation (see Rom. 1:20). So there certainly are similarities between man and animals. I gained valuable information when I read an article about the hierarchy of chimpanzees. A dominant male gains his position by fighting and intimidating the rest of the group. After dominance has been established, the male will strut around making gestures and noises to intimidate the other chimpanzees. What may seem strange, though, is that they actually encourage this behavior. His leadership provides order and security to the group.

This ritual not only serves the strongest male, giving him a place of prominence, but it also indicates to the others who will best protect them. Their sense of fearing the leader takes away their fear of other predators and enemies.

Another way for me to explain this idea is to use my own father as an example. When I was a young boy, I remember my father being very strong and authoritative. I respected him, and I feared him. Because I feared him, I never had to fear anyone else. I never had a problem going to sleep at night because I knew my father would take care of me. It is the same with God.

We must fear Him. According to Psalm 111:10, fear is the beginning of wisdom, and in fearing Him, we will not fear the enemy. Because I fear God, I'm not afraid. On the other hand, we must be careful not to misunderstand the concept of fear. First John 4:8 says that God is love. John continues in verse 18, "There is no fear in love; but perfect love casts out fear, because fear involves torment. But he who fears has not been made perfect in love." Human reasoning believes the way to peace is to eliminate the fear of God when just the opposite is true. By relying on our own wisdom, we nullify the power of God and become prey to the enemy. A reverential fear or respect of God combined with a knowledge of His mercy and grace removes any apprehension or dread from our relationship with Him. This is perfect love.

The enemies of the children of Israel would have no reason to respect a God whom they themselves did not fear, so God demonstrated Himself powerfully to His people before they entered the Promised Land. When the children of Israel began to sing about the fear of the Lord, it was heard throughout the land by all their enemies. After the crossing of the Red Sea, they sang, "Fear and dread will fall on them; by the greatness of Your arm they will be as still as a stone, till Your people pass over, O Lord, till the people pass over whom You have purchased" (Ex. 15:16). Fear in the hearts of their enemies ensured the Israelites of victory. Let us not think of God as only merciful and kind, but let us receive the whole counsel of God, believing in His awesome, almighty power and absolute authority.

With a strong God and strong leaders, we will become a strong people. As the children of Israel approached Canaan, the Bible says that the fear of them was upon every man and that their hearts melted with fear (see Josh. 5:1). Every nation feared the Israelites. They became an anointed and powerful people who entered the land of their inheritance. Without the element of fear, there can be no dominion. When the Lord gave Noah the mandate to take dominion of the earth, God said that the fear of him (Noah) would be upon every beast of the field and every fowl of the air (see Gen. 9:2). This, in turn, ensured his dominion.

We need to understand how the mandate given to Noah will be fulfilled in the Church. It will not happen by usurping authority like the chimpanzees; rather, promotion comes when we follow the principles of God. Jesus did not assume His place of authority by displaying His power; it was established because of His character. Isaiah 42:1-4 says:

Behold! My Servant whom I uphold...He will not cry out, nor raise His voice, nor cause His voice to be heard in the street. A bruised reed He will not break, and smoking flax He will not quench...He will not fail nor be discouraged, till He has established justice in the earth....

Jesus' obedience, character, and anointing brought Him promotion.

Our Giftings

As we review and examine the equipping ministries as outlined in Ephesians 4, we need to understand that although they are all equipping ministries, each ministry has different levels of authority. For example, many people today have the call of an apostle, yet their levels of authority are different. One may be called as an apostle to churches in a particular area or country, while another may be called as an apostle to the nations. Many people are gifted in one or all these five ministries; however, whether or not their gifting is received depends on the level of authority within the local church, their individual character, and the specific call of God upon their lives.

Gifts in themselves do not qualify a person for leadership. It is quite possible to be gifted in any or all of the equipping ministries without ever becoming a leader in the house of God. Many people refer to these gifts as offices, but the word *office* in the Scriptures refers to a function, not a position. Any position of authority will come because we have earned it by ministering to particular people or by authority delegated to us from the church or structure we are a part of.

Keeping this in mind, we can reexamine how we receive ministries, especially if they have tried to gain recognition because of their giftings. Verses 16 and 20 of Matthew 7 say that we would know and judge ministers by their fruit. Many people have been alienated from the Church because we have misunderstood their authority or have not recognized their gifting. We need to be cautious, especially those of us who are Charismatic, to follow the principles outlined in the Scriptures for choosing and honoring leadership if we do not want to be deceived.

In conclusion, we become the Bride of Christ collectively if we allow God's work to be completed in us individually. Our ultimate goal as Christians, however, is to become full-grown sons of God. Romans 8:19 reads, "For the earnest expectation of the creation eagerly waits for the revealing of the sons of God." Every believer's goal should be to become like Jesus Christ in fulfillment of Romans 8:29, "...that He might be the firstborn among many brethren."

Chapter 10

A House
for the Father

For years the Church has been a house of conformation —a place where people conform to religious law without being changed. God wants the Church to be a house of transformation—a place where people are changed by God's Spirit. The world conforms people to it, but God transforms people unto Himself and likeness. We are not to be conformed to this world, but transformed by the renewing of our minds (see Rom. 12:2). The Father is looking for sons who have been transformed, people who can face the challenges of this present generation.

Before the Church can ever become like Jesus Christ, she must see and understand Him as He is.

First John 3:2 says, "...it has not yet been revealed what we shall be, but we know that when He is revealed, we shall be like Him, for we shall see Him as He is." As Jesus was in the world, so are we to be in the world. Today, like no other time in the history of the Church, the Spirit is calling us to go on to full maturity, to that which the Father has purposed. "And this we will do if God permits" (Heb. 6:3). Now is God's time. He not only permits us, but calls us to fullness.

Perceiving the Father

Proverbs 1:8 says, "My son, hear the instruction of your father, and do not forsake the law of your mother." A father's greatest lessons come not by what he teaches directly to his children, but by what he lives before them. In Proverbs 31, the mother was the one who was close to the children in the home, not the father. He was at the gate with the elders tending to the affairs of the city. The children learned by his example, but what is more important, they were influenced by the mother in their thinking and attitude toward him. The mother is the one who is responsible for bringing forth children and presenting them to the father; her priority is to bring glory and honor to him. She understands the importance of reflecting a good image of the father to the children, so she does her utmost to reflect his love to them.

In John 5:19 Jesus said, "...the Son can do nothing of Himself, but what He sees the Father do; for whatever He does, the Son also does in like manner." How a child perceives his father affects and determines the kind of person he will grow up to be. If the mother does not speak well or project a good image of the father to the children, she will hinder them from becoming like him.

The Church has often damaged the children's perception of the Father. She has not provided a clear, true representation; their twisted image of God caused them to grow awkwardly. Therefore, she could not present mature children unto the Father. The Father's house must reveal the identity of the Father. The Church, however, has not recognized her proper role and presented sons to the Father after His image—she has formed disciples unto herself. The laws of the mother are to train and discipline the children as the father instructs. The children, in turn, are then able to submit to the chastisement of the father. "If you endure chastening, God deals with you as with sons..." (Heb. 12:7).

The Identity of Jesus Christ

If the Son could only do what He saw the Father do, then it is also necessary for the Church to have a visible demonstration of God's work. First we can consider Jesus Christ Himself, the visible and express image of the Father (see Heb. 1:3). If we want to see the Father, we need to look at Jesus. No fullness will come to us until we see the fullness of the Father in Him. Colossians 1:19 says of Jesus Christ, "...in Him all the fullness should dwell." We need to understand that although Jesus is a man and the true Son of God, He is also God.

Many conflicts have risen throughout Church history regarding the trinity of the Godhead. According to the Bible, the Trinity is a great mystery. The configuration of God is so far above our human reasoning that we could never totally comprehend who He is. However, we can understand that Jesus Christ, though He was fully man, was also fully God. We know that there are three distinct manifestations of God in the Father, Son, and Holy Ghost; yet we fully believe that the Lord our God is one God. When we see Jesus, we see the Father. When Philip asked to see the Father, Jesus replied, "Have I been with you so long, and yet you have not known Me, Philip? He who has seen Me has seen the Father..." (Jn. 14:9). Jesus was a visible image of the Father and He demonstrated His character.

Without this understanding, we tend to separate the God of the Old Testament from the God of the New Testament. We need a consistent revelation of God in the Old and the New Testaments to become fully acquainted with Him; otherwise, we will see Him as a cold and distant figure, one who is unapproachable and provokes fear. Although we must respect Him, we also need to see Him as a loving and caring Father. When Jesus told the Jews that Abraham rejoiced to see His day, they didn't believe that He, who was standing before them in human form, had actually seen Abraham. Jesus said to them in John 8:58, "Most assuredly, I say to you, before Abraham was, I AM." When Jesus said this, the Jews understood what He meant. He was saying that He was the God of Moses who revealed Himself as the I AM. This bold declaration caused them to take up stones to kill Him.

No wonder the enemy fights to stop people from truly knowing who Jesus is. Every cult has one doctrine in common; they do not believe in the deity of Jesus Christ. If you do not know Jesus as God, you will never know God as He really is. Jesus came to show us the character of God. The Old Testament revealed the person or character of God through the law, but the New Testament clearly reveals Him in Jesus Christ. The Old Testament shows us a type or shadow of Him, while the New Testament actually reveals His nature. When the Church sees the Father, as He is revealed in Jesus Christ, she will understand what it means to be like Him. Then she will fulfill the same function that Jesus did when He was on the earth; she will reveal the character and life of the Father to the world. Like Jesus, the Church should be a revelation of the Father, a visible expression of an invisible God.

The true identity of Jesus Christ is one of the foundational doctrines of the Church. In A.D. 325, the early Church fathers at the Council of Nicaea settled this issue once and for all. Jesus, though distinct from the Father, was begotten, not made; of one substance with the Father. Arius, like many cults today, claimed that the Son was completely separate from the Father. He did not believe that Jesus was a revelation of God and the Redeemer of mankind.

Demonstrating God's Character

When sons in the Father's house see the Father's true character demonstrated, they will begin to grow and mature, having that same character. This must first be demonstrated by those in leadership in the house of God. Ministers and ministries must provide a visible expression of the Father to the Body. Where do the children look for leadership if there is no visible demonstration in the house? This principle not only applies to the house of God, it also applies in our individual households as well.

In the home, the father holds a place of authority that results from his character, not his position. Children ruled under authority without love become bitter and rebellious. They may show loyalty outwardly to their father, but they certainly feel no love for him. Similarly, in the Church, we've seen a superficial form of Christianity; many people lack real commitment. As fathers in the house begin to visibly demonstrate God's true character, the entire house will become like Him. The Father's character revealed through the fruit of the Spirit in believers will change the world.

Because of the visible image of Jesus Christ, we can personally know who God is, not just see His acts. God wants to reveal Himself to the world today. Many Old Testament testimonies revealed what God could do, but Jesus came to show us who God is. Only God could bear witness of Himself. Today, because of the power of the cross, we can bear witness to His person. The ongoing work of the Holy Spirit is to produce or perform the work of Christ in us. Paul wrote in Galatians 4:19, "My little children, for whom I labor in birth again until Christ is formed in you." When we first come to Christ, we receive His divine seed; it should then grow and mature until it ripens as the fruit of the Holy Spirit. The characteristics of this fruit are demonstrated in the life of Jesus Christ and is nothing less than the Father's own character revealed first in Christ and now in us.

It is time for the Pentecostal and Charismatic Movements to change their focus. The gifts of the Spirit are not to be our emphasis. Gifts are the beginning, but Paul also says, "If we live in the Spirit, let us also walk in the Spirit" (Gal. 5:25). If you have experienced spiritual life, it is time to develop a spiritual walk. This walk should be a visible demonstration of the Father's character to the world. The world not only needs to hear the gospel, they also need to see it. Christians should be living epistles known and read of all men (see 2 Cor. 3:2).

An Improper Basis for Ministry

Pentecostal and Charismatic Christians have received ministries and granted them authority based upon their gifts, completely disregarding their fruit. As we discussed before, Jesus said that we would know people by their fruit (Mt. 7:20). Fruit represents the development of the character of Christ in a person. When we bear fruit, we become a living demonstration of Christ in the earth. Only then, as stated in Revelation, will the vine be ripe for harvest (see Rev. 14:18). The Husbandman of the earth, the Father, has the long patience necessary to see it. He will send the early and the latter rain (see Joel 2:23). Remember, Jesus said, "I am the true vine, and My Father is the vinedresser. Every branch in Me that does not bear fruit He takes away; and every branch that bears fruit He prunes, that it may bear more fruit" (Jn. 15:1-2). Jesus told His disciples that if they would abide in Him, they would bear much fruit, and by this, the Father is glorified (see Jn. 15:4,8). It is from this fruit that the new wine will flow.

Look again at the equipping ministries in Ephesians 4. This reference speaks about gifts, but it also refers to people who have grown into full stature as sons of God. Ministries cannot bring people to maturity if they themselves are not mature. Many Pentecostal and Charismatic groups have suffered disillusionment about the authority of these ministries because they have not understood the principles involved in maturity. People have been promoted to places of authority simply because of their gifts, and the results have been disastrous.

I repeat, individuals do not qualify for a ministry or position based on their multiplicity of gifts. Although it seems right that a prophet be gifted in all of the revelation gifts, we violate Jesus' instructions to judge people by their fruit if we judge them by their gifts. A false prophet may have many gifts and a large following of people, but this does not make him less false; it only makes him more dangerous. Examining fruit implies that we must get close to someone, have a relationship with them, and be able to witness the character of Christ in their lives. Thus a standard for judging true fathers in the house is relationship.

Other ministries have been established based upon their rank or comparative standing. For example, those ministers who have the gift of prophecy would not be esteemed as highly as those who have the office of a prophet. This process of comparison is against the teachings of Paul in First Corinthians 12. One gift is not more important than others. Each gift is vital to the whole.

Remember, the word *office* is not a scriptural term. When the word is used in the Bible, the original intent or meaning does not refer to a position or office, but to the function of a person. In fact, there is no corresponding word in the original Greek. Usually the same Greek word is repeated. A better translation would be the diaconate of a deacon or service of a servant. We need to return to biblical principles concerning fatherhood ministries.

Neither is the Father's house a political structure, even though many religious institutions have strived to make it one over the years. When a church esteems one person over another because of his gift, it only divides the congregation and causes some to think more highly of themselves. The leading or direction of the church does not come because of power; it comes because of authority. It is God who works authority in an individual as he consistently maintains faithfulness of character in the Father's house. This is why church leaders should not be elected, but divinely planted and developed in the house. If they are producing proper fruit, it will be witnessed by others. The local leaders and church body will see the fruit growing and know the gifting or function of an individual as he lives before the people. A church cannot err if it follows this principle.

Coming to Maturity

If someone has allowed God to work in his life and he has fully matured, he qualifies for fatherhood. It's disastrous when children try to be fathers. Even the most intelligent or gifted individual will fail if he is not mature. This principle seems simple enough, yet many people who should know better, people who should be living by Kingdom principles, overlook it. As a church fully matures, fathers will begin to emerge. These are great and glorious days because the Church is learning to walk in full authority.

In First Corinthians 13:10-11, Paul wrote, "But when that which is perfect has come, then that which is in part will be done away. When I was a child, I spoke as a child, I understood as a child, I thought as a child; but when I became a man, I put away childish things." Childish things or *toys* are imitations or downscaled versions of the real thing. When that which is perfect has come, the *toys* will pass away. Contrary to what most dispensationalists teach, this does not mean that when the written Word came, there was no longer the need for spiritual gifts. Paul was talking about the development of the fullness of the gifts. When we were children, we knew in part and prophesied in part, but when that which is perfect is come, then that which is in part will be gone. In other words, when we are mature, we will function in the fullness of our gifts.

To have all the gifts operating to their full potential in a church, we must individually walk in fullness. The word *perfect* in this context does not mean someone who is flawless, but who is complete. It speaks of someone who has reached his full potential in God, walking totally in His will. Hebrews 5:9 talks about Jesus having been made perfect. We know that from the beginning, He was the spotless and unblemished Lamb of God. If He had not been sinless, He couldn't have been offered as the sacrifice for all sin. He was made perfect by totally surrendering to the will of the heavenly Father. When He surrendered His own will, He was made complete. This is what the Father looks for—our total surrender—so His will can be accomplished in us.

The Father's standard of holiness has been compromised far too long. Leaders must stop making excuses for their own failures. We have experienced God's grace and power to forgive, but it's time to raise the standard and become true examples of Christ. God has certainly set very high standards for His leaders in the Word.

Commitment to the People

True obedience to the Father will only be accomplished through dying to self and this, of course, is painful. Jesus, although He was a son, learned obedience by the things that He suffered. Most leaders today do not want to pay the high price for leadership; God's leaders must die to self and live for God. A parent who raises good strong children is willing to suffer and make sacrifices for them. We must be willing to bear the reproach of Christ and enter into His sufferings to achieve these standards.

Moses is a wonderful example because the Scriptures say that when he came of age, he refused to be called Pharaoh's son, esteeming the reproach of Christ greater than the riches of Egypt (see Heb. 11:24-26). He chose to suffer affliction with the people of God rather than enjoy the passing pleasures of sin. The Father longs for leaders who have a heart to serve His people, who are willing to pay the price.

Moses, said to have been the meekest man to ever live, was a man of great authority (see Num. 12:3). According to the Scriptures, no other man had more authority with God or men than Moses. The Levites rose up against him in rebellion and God defended Moses by causing the earth to open up and swallow them (see Num. 16). When his own family murmured against him, God's wrath fell on them. Miriam was stricken with leprosy for challenging his authority (see Num. 12).

The Church today does not walk in this kind of authority. There is a lack of commitment in leadership and in the people to the call of God. When I first made the decision to begin training for the ministry, I had sensed the call of God on my life and, while in prayer, God spoke a tremendous word to me. He said, "If you will suffer with Christ, you will also be glorified together with Him." Suffering in itself does not bring spiritual authority. God did not call us to a rigid life of asceticism. He wants to set His glory on us as we rule and reign together with Him. If we follow Him and commit to a Christian life—although we may suffer because of the choices we make—like Moses, our suffering will bring reward. We will receive authority in our Father's house.

The purpose of suffering is not simply for our personal sanctification. It is what we experience as a result of committing ourselves to ministry or the service of Christ to His people. Moses didn't just make a commitment to live a holy life; he made a commitment to live a life of service to the people of God. Priesthood ministry does not come without great authority from the Father. The life of Moses testifies that to truly lead God's people, one must receive great authority from God. The level of authority directly relates to how much we submit to the work of the ministry, both in service to the Father and in service to His people.

The writer to the Hebrews tried to explain this truth to them, but they were too spiritually immature to receive it. He wrote to them about Melchizedek, who was first mentioned in Genesis 14, saying that he was not only a priest, but also a king. He wrote that Jesus was a priest after the order of Melchizedek. (See Hebrews 6:20–7:28.) God wants us to walk in this same king/priest order of ministry today. We not only need to have the heart of a priest reaching out to the needs of the people, but we also need to walk in authority as a king, delivering people from bondage.

The Ministry of the Son

The name *Melchizedek* means king of righteousness. The Bible declares that the scepter of God's Kingdom is righteousness (see Heb. 1:8). The authority of this Kingdom comes when we learn submission.

Jesus did not struggle with those who sought to take His life; His struggle was submitting to the Father's will. If we perceive our struggle to be around us instead of acknowledging that it is within us, we will never gain authority in God.

When Jesus began His ministry on earth, following John the Baptist, He introduced the ministry of the Son. In Matthew 11:12 Jesus said, "And from the days of John the Baptist until now the kingdom of heaven suffers violence and the violent take it by force." Many people, when interpreting this verse, have stressed the importance of taking the Kingdom by force. They have not examined the rest of this statement—*until now*. Jesus was ushering in a new day. The ministry of the Son, in contrast to the ministry of John the Baptist, was immediate and drastic. John preached a forceful message of repentance, "neither eating or drinking." Jesus, on the other hand, came in peace, "eating and drinking." (See Matthew 11:18-19.) He did not point His finger to condemn, but reached out His hands in compassion.

"Come to Me, all you who labor and are heavy laden, and I will give you rest. Take My yoke upon you and learn from Me, for I am gentle and lowly in heart, and you will find rest for your souls. For My yoke is easy and My burden is light" (Matthew 11:28-30).

God has indeed called us to peace. Hebrews 7:2 says that Melchizedek was also the king of Salem, which is interpreted king of peace. Jesus did not follow the route normally taken by a king because His was no ordinary kingdom. The Bible says that His Kingdom is not eating or drinking, but righteousness, peace and joy in the Holy Ghost (see Rom. 14:17). Jesus walked in peace and righteousness. The Scriptures say,

...that Jesus...for the joy that was set before Him endured the cross, despising the shame, and has sat down at the right hand of the throne of God. For consider Him who endured such hostility from sinners against Himself, lest you become weary and discouraged in your souls. You have not yet resisted to bloodshed, striving against sin (Hebrews 12:2-4).

God will pour out the oil of gladness on those committed to righteousness, those who minister as kings/ priests after the order of Melchizedek.

But to the Son He says: "Your throne, O God, is forever and ever; a scepter of righteousness is the scepter of Your kingdom. You have loved righteousness and hated lawlessness; therefore God, Your God, has anointed You with the oil of gladness more than Your companions" (Hebrews 1:8-9).

The word *Salem* in the original Greek is also translated to mean complete, made ready, perfect, and quiet. This speaks about those who, like Jesus, have been made perfect or complete. The Scriptures say that Job was a perfect man because he loved God and hated evil (see Job 1:1). He proved his love for God by committing himself to what was right even in the midst of adversity. He was a witness to both the natural and spiritual worlds.

Jesus was willing to do the will of the Father and was obedient unto death, defeating the powers of darkness. Hear the call of the Father and make a commitment to righteousness.

This hope we have as an anchor of the soul, both sure and steadfast, and which enters the Presence behind the veil, where the forerunner has entered for us, even Jesus, having become High Priest forever according to the order of Melchizedek (Hebrews 6:19-20).

Jesus is our example of the perfect harmony of these distinct ministries. As the Son of God, He walked as a king having full authority to operate in the supernatural realm. As the Son of Man, Jesus walked among the people as a priest, showing them the Father in a way they could relate to.

In A.D. 451, the Council of Chalcedon decreed that not only was Jesus established as truly God and of one substance with the Father concerning His divinity, He was also truly man and of one substance with man concerning His humanity. With this greater understanding, we can fully see how the Church can demonstrate the same ministry as Jesus Christ in the earth today. The Charismatic and Pentecostal Movements have experienced divine empowerment through the Holy Spirit, but it is now necessary that we relate the spiritual life to our everyday walk.

According to Galatians 5:25, if we are going to live in the Spirit, we are also to walk in the Spirit. As we begin to reach out to our fellow man, our spiritual authority will be made complete. This explains why we are to judge men by their fruit and not by their gifts. It is then that proper balance will be established within the Church and the world will be able to relate to us. By dwelling in the Church, God can again live among the people.

Today God is revealing Himself as Father. Pray to receive a revelation of who He is and who you are. As God was in Christ reconciling the world unto Himself, so He will again do the same through the Church. The Spirit is calling people to full maturity. The Melchizedek priesthood will again be made manifest in the earth.

Chapter 11

The House of David

When we understand that Jesus was both human and divine, we can begin to see our ministry as sons of God in the earth. Jesus, the Son of God and the Son of Man, was also known as the Son of David because God's promised Son would come through David's seed.

The Son of David

In Ezekiel 34 the prophet of the Lord addressed the shepherds or leaders of the house of Israel. They had not fulfilled their divine commission to feed, heal, and care for the sheep of the Lord. Instead, they had ruled them by force and cruelty. They were more concerned about their own needs than those of the sheep. (Ezekiel also reproved the sheep. They too had become self-centered and were no longer concerned about the needs of the rest of the flock.) Therefore God, through the prophet Ezekiel, said He would raise up His servant David to feed and care for the sheep (see Ezek. 34:23). God said He would make a covenant of peace with them, make them and all the hills surrounding them a blessing, and make the house of the Lord a place of fruitfulness (see Ezek. 34:25-29). This prophecy was spoken many years after David died; therefore, we need to understand that David was a type or shadow of things to come.

This prophecy is Messianic in nature and speaks about the ministry of Jesus Christ, the Son of David. As we allow the character of Christ to be formed in us, we too become sons of David in the world. However, we need to meditate on the Scriptures concerning the Son of David. In Mark 12:35-37, Jesus asked the Jews while He taught in the temple, "How is it that the scribes say that the Christ is the Son of David? For David himself said by the Holy Spirit: 'The Lord said to my Lord, Sit at My right hand, till I make Your enemies Your footstool.' " Jesus asked them, in effect, "If He was truly the Son of David, then why did David call Him Lord?" They believed that the Messiah would come as the Son of David only from a natural viewpoint. Jesus showed them their need for enlightenment or revelation. We today also need spiritual vision.

The Example of David's Life

The Church today is the spiritual heritage of David, heir to all the blessings of his house. Many truths about our covenant with God are revealed to us through David's life. David was a man after God's own heart (see Acts 13:22). His relationship with God was special.

Although Jesus led a flawless life as our perfect example, David's life was more like our own—his heart was tender toward God, but he did not always display a perfect life style. David was someone we can readily identify with as we fulfill our desire to grow in stature and in the fullness of Christ.

When I received the laying on of hands with prophecy during the graduation service of Minister's Candidate School, the Lord told me my calling was like David's. I was to walk softly before Him, guarding the word spoken over me. Many things that God worked in David's life are important to me because God has worked them in my own life. In the same way, my experiences are not unique; they apply to many others in the house of the Father.

It was God who chose David for service. Men usually choose by outward appearance, but God always chooses by looking at the heart. When God sent Samuel to the house of Jesse to select a king over Israel, young David was not the logical choice. Any one of his older brothers seemed a better choice. David worked as a shepherd tending his father's sheep. David's availability and willingness to serve his natural father was evidence of his heart attitude. (See First Samuel 16.) Indeed, by their fruit you shall know them.

David's heart and life reflect his faithfulness, even in the small jobs he was asked to do. He could rest assured that his heavenly Father could open any door of opportunity for him. Isaiah referred to it as the key of

David, or the key that will open doors no man can shut and close doors no man can open (see Is. 22:22). David's heart was filled with faith that God would work on his behalf. He never struggled for a position or place of service in God because he knew it was God who appointed them. He simply became a faithful servant, even taking the job of a humble shepherd. But David was a man of destiny. The heavenly Father had a destiny or purpose for him. God opened the door that led David directly to the throne of his nation. God took the kingdom from Saul and gave it to David.

What Ezekiel saw in David is a type or example for the Church. Just as Ezekiel prophesied, God raised up David His servant to bring change to the nation. What an impact the Church would have in the world if every individual in the house of the Father had a heart like David's and served to the best of his ability, not worrying about promotion or personal glory! The flock would respond differently to one another and place their confidence in God rather than in seeking a reward at the expense of others.

Many people have been hurt, especially new Christians, because of political posturing in the house. When the Church understands, like David, that promotion comes from God, the driving need to push each other out of the way to make room for ourselves will be eliminated. David's heart was set on serving, not leading. Our desire to work for God must be built upon this principle. The Father is seeking those who have a heart that desires to serve Him.

When Saul lost the anointing and was vexed by an evil spirit, he called for David to comfort him by playing the harp. At this point in David's life, the servants of Saul described him as a skillful musician, a mighty man of valor, a man of war, prudent in speech, handsome, and someone whom the Lord was with (see 1 Sam. 16:18). He was very well known. Next, David was appointed as armor bearer. God placed him to serve the king he had been anointed and called to replace. God was promoting David without him doing anything to make it happen.

One of David's greatest moments of triumph came on the day he delivered food to his brothers who were fighting against the Philistines. A nine-foot giant named Goliath had challenged the army of Israel, but there was no man to stand against him. When David inquired about the situation, his brothers demeaned him by asking why he was not tending his sheep.

Unfortunately, whenever someone tries to do something for God, people often question his motives or put him down. David, though, was not swayed by his brothers' comments. He stood up for the cause of the Lord and volunteered to fight the giant. God had delivered a lion and a bear into his hands when they attacked his father's sheep; so without any doubt, God could deliver Goliath into his hands. David defeated Goliath and became a man of great reputation and high honor before the people. Thus those who have proven themselves faithful servants in the house of the Father will receive promotion.

Likewise, as I have remained faithful to God, doing whatever He has asked me to do, He has opened doors of opportunity for me. I have never had to make a way for myself. Obedience to God is the only thing that qualifies us for His blessing. A servant does not make choices—a servant does what his Master says. As we become servants of our Father, our confidence is placed in Him who holds our future.

Rest in God's Plan

You are a person of destiny. God has charted a plan for your life. Each one whose name is written in the Book of Life must realize that God has written the *story line* of his life (see Ps. 69:28; Phil. 4:3; Rev. 3:5). If we are obedient, God guarantees our place in the Book and we can rest in His perfect will. Because we are people of destiny, we should never feel threatened or protective of our places of ministry. God has an individual plan and purpose for each of us. This plan is designed not only to bless us, but also to make us a blessing. God is a God of eternal purpose; we were in Christ before the foundations of the world (see Eph. 1:4). Many people forget that nothing happens by chance. Because we know that God ultimately owns, knows, and controls all things, we can submit to one another, to civil government, or any other area of authority. These are all His ministers for good.

God taught me this principle in a unique way. I knew we would outgrow our first location on a four-acre parcel of land located about one mile off an interstate highway. I had always felt that we should try to get land closer to the highway to be more visible to the community. Located west of the highway was a vacant parcel of land that I considered ideal for future expansion. But one day the Lord told me to go to the property on the other side of the highway. It was not considered prime property, but wetland, and was located on a dirt road.

As I obeyed the Lord and walked along the border of the property by the highway, I found an old *For Sale* sign under the weeds. When I got home, my wife informed me that Mary Warren had called. Mary and I had become acquainted through Minister's Candidate School. She has a ministry of intercession and has prayed for me several times. When I returned her call, Mary explained that while interceding for me in prayer, the Lord told her to specifically tell me to "go in and take the land." I knew at this point I was walking into a prepared inheritance.

When I called the realtor about the property, he told me they had been trying to sell it for years, and that no one had ever made an offer to purchase it. He assured me that the owners would be glad to sell and quite possibly the price could be negotiated. That Sunday, I asked my congregation to pray about purchasing the property because it would require a walk of faith. A few days later I was looking at the property again and trying to imagine how it might accommodate us. I was meditating on the word that the Lord had spoken concerning the church being a city set on a hill. As I walked up to the top of a hill, I saw some people planting trees on the property. I was surprised to see them and even more surprised when they said that they were the new owners. They had recently purchased 10 acres of a 52-acre parcel and stated another couple had just purchased 10 more acres.

I called the realtor and he also was surprised to find out that the property had indeed been sold. He informed me that there were still 32 acres available if I were interested. However, the remaining property did not border the highway and in order to access it, one would have to travel down a dirt road. I told the realtor that I was not interested and simply went to God about the need, for as far as I was concerned, those people were planting trees on our property. A few weeks later the realtor called and said that the couple who bought the property were transferred to New Jersey. He exclaimed, "Can you imagine, they planted 1,100 trees on that property!" It wasn't long until Mt. Zion Temple owned the entire 52-acre parcel and a thousand plus trees, and began building a new sanctuary.

Possessing What God Has Given

At that time the Lord began revealing to me that we are a people of destiny. Even more specifically, He showed me that we were a people of manifest destiny. Manifest destiny motivated the early settlers of America. They believed that coming to America to establish a free land was ordained by God; therefore, they were willing to face adversity. They believed that since the mandate came from God, they would succeed. Manifest destiny inspired the Puritans to believe they had a mandate from God to possess and develop the new world. Although this does not excuse the way they dispossessed the Native Americans, God's hand was in the settlement of the Americas. Since then the United States has been a force for evangelism used by God to reach the whole world.

Dispossession is a biblical principle. The right to dispossess motivated the children of Israel to go in and take the Promised Land. God took the land away from the Canaanites and gave it to the Israelites, allowing them to possess a great inheritance.

We get disturbed when we hear people say that God will give us something that belongs to someone else because the Scriptures tell us that we are not to covet. But Psalm 24:1 says, "The earth is the Lord's, and all its fullness, the world and those who dwell therein." God owns all things; He has the right to declare ownership of anything on earth. People are just stewards of those things. The principle of stewardship is one of the greatest determining forces of what happens in the world. We can lose possession of something if we become careless stewards.

God informed the children of Israel that He had the right to dispossess the people of the land of Canaan. If they believed and recognized this, they would go into the land with great faith. It didn't matter if giants lived there because God had told them it was their land; they had a right to it. When the Lord gives one person something, at the same time He dispossesses someone else. If we believe this today, our faith will increase and we will become more aware of our stewardship responsibilities.

Many events in the world today are the results of improper stewardship. For example, when the Iron Curtain toppled in Eastern Europe, many people declared it to be the victory of capitalism over communism, the victory of the United States over the Soviet Union. However, a closer examination of the Word reveals that the Lord is just exercising His option to lift up or to tear down. It follows, then, that if the United States refuses to keep His commandments, we will see the same thing occur here. Power is not in a system, but in the sanctification of the people.

Dispossession also is clearly demonstrated in the story of Shebna and Eliakim in Isaiah 22. The Lord sent a message from the prophet to Shebna, a steward of high position and authority, that God was going to remove him from his office and Eliakim would take his place. Shebna had become proud in his accomplishments and had even built a sepulcher in his own honor. The Lord declared that He would strip Shebna of his accomplishments, and he would have to watch as Eliakim gained his possessions and exercised his authority. God said that Shebna's honor would go to Eliakim and that he would be known as a father in the land in Shebna's place.

It is difficult to lose something precious, but it's far more humiliating to see someone else possess it. The laws of sowing and reaping and stewardship go hand in hand, reinforcing God's will in the earth. God told Eliakim that he would receive the key of David, a key that would enable him to open doors no man could shut and close doors no man could open (see Is. 22:22). This authority comes from God and can only be taken away by Him. This key also is promised to the church of Philadelphia in Revelation 3:8, and provides power and confidence. This church has little strength, yet still serves God. God, in turn, will open doors of opportunity that no one can close and give that church the key of David.

When Saul lost the anointing, seeing David with it literally drove him crazy. He was tormented by a demon and lived the remainder of his life without God's blessing, knowing that someone else had his honor. David then gained possession of Saul's kingdom. This horrible dispossession illustrates God's wisdom and purpose. It demonstrates God's faithfulness to His anointed while showing the result of sin and disobedience. The consequences of sin are devastating; yet they serve a profound purpose—to teach valuable lessons.

David understood that the key to all blessing was in the Lord's hands. He never fought against Saul. Even when David had reason and opportunity to kill Saul, he refused to touch God's anointed. He knew that in God's time everything would fall into place according to His purpose and that he must simply keep his integrity. David had a heart after God. He received what had belonged to another, but he never took it by force. This principle is also apparent in the story of Shebna and Eliakim. Eliakim did not strive to achieve another's possessions; he did not covet them. He simply received what the Lord had given him. Shebna built for himself, while Eliakim, whose name is interpreted *God will raise him up,* was a servant unto the Lord.

Responding to the Problems of Stewardship

Today many companies are being challenged; their very existence hangs in the balance because of improper stewardship. The state of Michigan's economy is heavily influenced by the automobile industry; General Motors, Ford, and Chrysler have attained tremendous power and impacted the nation. However, during the 1970's, the executives of these companies began to neglect their stewardship responsibilities. They believed that their success and good fortune would never change. When the government started lifting restrictions, many foreign companies began competing for business. Consumers soon discovered that foreign-made automobiles were better built. Our companies continued running unprofitable plants and received tax breaks, but when the Reagan administration ended benefits, they were faced with the long-term effects of improper stewardship.

Many people affiliated with the automobile industry literally hate Japanese people because of their perceived threat to the economy. In the past, this was the "stuff" wars were made of; precipitated by a covetous spirit. However, rather than blame someone else for our misfortune, we should first seek to restore our integrity concerning stewardship. Don't blame people around you for the problem or be consumed with hatred. Seek repentance. When we do well, we will find acceptance.

When people in ministry lose sight of their role as servants, they are called upon to give an account of their stewardship. Judgment has been pronounced when they begin to lose what God has placed in their hands. If a local church's account has been found wanting, this judgment process will begin. First, God withdraws His anointing. Then people begin to leave. At this point, instead of seeking God to find out why people are leaving, the leaders begin to find fault with the churches that are growing. They start preaching against people changing churches, forgetting that there was a time when people left other churches to come to theirs. The people who choose to stay do so out of loyalty and commitment. It's sad to see the tactics these leaders use to keep people once the anointing is gone.

The servants of the Lord must realize that there are times when God simply realigns things. Many times, in order for God to fulfill His purpose, everything in our lives will seem to be in disorder or upheaval. This can be very disconcerting and many times, without realizing it, we rise up in rebellion against God. During these times, we must keep our hearts soft toward Him so we will not work against Him. David always sought God in important matters because he knew it was necessary, as God's servant, to be close to Him when making decisions. Keeping close to Him not only opens the door to full obedience, but also gives us the ability to learn what God is speaking to us in our situation.

We at Mt. Zion Temple learned this in the second stage of our building program. When our church had finally purchased the 52 acres, the next step was to draw up building plans based upon the vision given by

God. The first plan included a 52,000-square foot building. When we presented the plans to the township for their review, they blatantly disapproved. The board said they did not want us or our building in their township. After they said many demeaning things about the church and slammed the door in our face, I was filled with righteous indignation. They were not going to stop me from doing what God told me to do! I decided it was time to fight, so I encouraged the church to gather signatures for a petition and we held a demonstration in the front of the town hall to show them our strength and determination. I was ready for battle—but then God spoke.

Let every soul be subject to the governing authorities. For there is no authority except from God, and the authorities that exist are appointed by God. Therefore whoever resists the authority resists the ordinance of God, and those who resist will bring judgment on themselves (Romans 13:1-2).

The Lord reminded me of His word about government. Government is for our good and if we resist government, we resist God. This was a shocking revelation to me. When I thought I was doing the will of God, I was resisting Him. I needed an altar of repentance because I did not have the heart of David. I had not been willing to suffer, trusting God, but resisted the authority over me. I confessed this to the church and proceeded with a new agenda to fulfill the Father's will.

I met with the township supervisor and asked what I could do to change the situation and began working with the township instead of against them. The supervisor told me to downsize the original plan, as requested by the planning commission, and then to proceed as approvals were given. He said that if we'd follow their direction, once we were on the property, we'd be able to modify the plans as needed. When I presented the revised plan to the commission, it was approved, but the planning commission kept us under close observation.

They decided the number of windows, the size of the building, the kind of siding, the number of shrubs, etc. They controlled almost every phase of construction. It wasn't easy keeping silent, but the Father was teaching me a lesson. He wanted me to know that all authority indeed comes from Him and to believe that the government was a ministry of good and not evil. Romans 13:5 says, "Therefore you must be subject, not only because of wrath but also for conscience' sake." The Father dealt with the issues of my heart.

Since then I have learned that God uses government to place building plans and expansions on a timetable for our good. Timing is such an important factor in God. When you walk His way, you walk in assurance because lasting results hinge upon proper timing. Man always builds for an immediate need, while God builds for a future one. When we understand that the Father's house is the house of David, the servant with a faithful heart, and give Him rule over our hearts, we are guaranteed continued success.

Chapter 12

A House of Rest

My early days of ministry were quite stressful, not because of the ministry, but because of my character. I was immature. God had many things to work into my character before I could be comfortable as a co-laborer with Him. It can be very trying working with someone totally different from yourself and because I had always been such an anxious person, it added to the difficulty.

Even when I was a child, I worried about everything. If I'd hear my parents talking about hard economic times or a possible strike, I'd worry. When I listened to news reports, I'd worry about nuclear war and injustice. I knew there would be civil war because of the racial upheaval of the day. If my parents were out late, I was certain they'd been in an accident. Every time someone in the family got sick, I was sure it would be fatal. Even at church, I worried about the great tribulation and the antichrist. I worried about everything.

As a small boy, I felt the call of God on my life and, being from a missionary-minded church, I remember telling my mother that I wanted to be a missionary when I grew up. My mother was so proud. She shared this with our pastor and he always referred to me as his little missionary. However, when I heard about people being killed on the mission field, I was terrified. What could I do? Instead of becoming a missionary, I decided I could better serve the Lord as a deacon. When my older sister, Jeanne, went away to college, she wrote home to tell me that in psychology class she had been studying about different types of per-sonalities. She said, from the descriptions she had reviewed, that she felt I was neurotic. I didn't ap-preciate her diagnosis, but I knew she was right.

I started in ministry when I was just 24 years old. Not only did I face the rigors of ministry, I also under-stood the responsibility of the call God had placed on my life. I knew the Lord had spoken multiplication and increase, so naturally I expected immediate growth. After the church had started, my brother, Bill, counted 37 people one Sunday morning and commented, "I thought God told you a lot of people were going to come!" He only expressed what I had been thinking. I too wondered how God's promise would ever come to pass.

A Man of Rest

One day as I worried in prayer before the Lord, He spoke a profound word to my spirit: "I have chosen the man of rest to build my house." This word pertains to David (see 1 Chron. 17:3-15). David summoned Nathan the prophet to his home and told him he desired to build a house for God. David had just completed the construction of his own home and thought that God should have one also. He had achieved peace around the borders of Israel and was ready to do something special for God.

Nathan agreed it was a noble thing to do and encouraged David, but the Lord told Nathan that He had not asked David to build His house and that he could not do it. David was a man of war and had shed much blood, so God said he could not build His house (see 1 Chron. 22:8). Instead, God promised to raise up a son who would be a man of rest. God said, "He shall build Me a house, and I will establish his throne forever" (1 Chron. 17:12). During the reign of David's son, Solomon, Israel was given rest from all her enemies. The name *Solomon* means rest or peace.

Obedience: Better Than Sacrifice

Four important lessons can be learned from this narrative. First, the Lord didn't want David to build His house because He did not tell him to. A big mistake Christians make is to assume that God accepts anything we offer. The Word makes it clear that God will only receive what He asks for. Samuel prophesied to King Saul, "To obey is better than sacrifice" (1 Sam. 15:22). Saul offered something that God did not ask for and it cost him the kingdom. Presumption is thinking that God will automatically accept what we offer. He is a sovereign, omnipotent God and will not settle for anything less than what He requires of us.

This is exemplified in the sacrifices offered by Cain and Abel. Many Bible scholars have speculated as to why God accepted one offering and not the other. One thing is sure—Abel offered his firstfruits, his sacrifice, by faith (see Gen. 4:4; Heb. 11:4), while Cain offered what he wanted to. God requires firstfruits. The first and best is what God specifically reserved for Himself; anything else is second best.

When we offer something that we think belongs to us, something that God did not ask for, we actually deny His ownership of all things. In the Word, the principle of tithing is based upon the premise that everything belongs to God. When someone gives his tithe, he acknowledges God's sovereign ownership of all things. When we realize we are only stewards, our hearts' desire is to please the Lord. We give what He asks.

If we honestly believe that God is really who He says—omniscient, omnipresent, omnipotent, etc.— what could we possibly offer Him that He doesn't already have? It is ridiculous to think that we have something God needs. God is complete in Himself and simply allows us to participate in His eternal plan. It is no wonder that the sacrifices God prefers are, as David declares in Psalm 51:17, a broken spirit and a contrite heart. These sacrifices He will not despise.

Many Christians do not understand that they have nothing to offer. Some judge and compare the worth of their sacrifices. Jesus told the legalistic people of His

178

day to study the Scriptures that said God would rather have mercy than sacrifice (see Mt. 9:13). When we give from a contrite and broken heart, honoring the almighty God, our attitude is very different. We are grateful that God reached out to us to save us from our sin. Ephesians 2:1 says, "And you He made alive, who were dead in trespasses and sins." If we would only realize our lack and see His abundance, we would so easily place our confidence in Him.

God: Our Source

In order to become people of rest, the second lesson we need to learn is that everything belongs to God; He is our source of supply. The only thing of substance that we can build for God is what we build according to His design, from the resources that He has supplied. Psalm 127:1a says, "Unless the Lord builds the house, they labor in vain who build it."

When God placed Adam in the garden, He provided everything Adam would ever need to accomplish the Father's will. God always supplies the resources to accomplish what He asks us to do. Before Solomon ever began building the temple, his father David had already made the provision for it (see 1 Chron. 28). God abundantly blessed Solomon with rest as he ascended the throne. This is the pattern God wants for us.

After God told David that he couldn't build Him a temple, an interesting turn of events took place. God said that He was going to build David a house. When we understand that we have nothing to offer God and that He owns everything, we will discover that God wants to bless us more than we can imagine.

At this point, King David had obviously lost sight of his humble beginnings. Earlier in his life, when he faced Goliath the great Philistine, David knew beyond any doubt that it was God that would give him the victory. Whenever we arrive at a comfortable stage in our walk with God, we are tempted to lose our confidence in Him.

If we forget who the Author of our faith is, we forget who the Finisher is as well (see Heb. 12:2). God had been with David all the days of his life. He had been a mere shepherd boy when God chose him and anointed him to be king. He wasn't one whom men would have chosen, but God looked at his heart. God had cut off all his enemies and given him a name like no other on the earth: God promised to not only bless David, but also his seed after his death. When we die to ourselves, Jesus said that we receive His life (see Lk. 9:23-24). Our efforts must die before God's power is revealed.

Through the years, many leaders have urged people to do something for God. Like Nathan, most of us would immediately encourage others to do something for God. We must become more sensitive to the Holy Spirit because success in ministry only comes by hearing God. No wonder the Word says, "He who has an ear to hear, let him hear what the Spirit says to the churches" (i.e., Rev. 2:7). The carnal mind cannot comprehend the work of the Holy Spirit. We must be renewed in the spirit of our mind.

By examining the Scriptures closely, you will see that it has always been God's desire to do something for us. When God first created Adam, He gave him dominion over all the works of His hands. In the midst of creation, God provided something unique and special for man, the garden of Eden. The word *Eden* means delightsome land and voluptuous living. It would provide everything mankind would need; there was no better place. It has always been God's desire to bless man.

His Ability, Not Ours

The third lesson to learn is that God is the One who enables us to build. David learned that his success was not dependent upon the ability that he had received from the Father's hand, but on the ability of God. We cannot be people of rest if we rely on our own abilities. Our confidence must always be in God and in His ability to perform the work He commissions. We must be persuaded that He is able to keep what we have committed unto Him (see 2 Tim. 1:12). When David acted independently of God, he became a man of war, tainted with blood guilt and this disqualified him for the building of the temple. We must be careful not to become self-sufficient or the end result will be death.

God Is in Control

The final principle is to know that God is in complete control. All power belongs to Him. We must be a people who surrenders to God. When we try to take control, we worry and attempt to resolve circumstances. A person of rest is one who surrenders everything to the Father. We cannot rest when we try to take control. Jesus is the Prince of Peace and wherever He reigns, there is peace.

When God designed the universe, He gave order to everything. As long as the order was maintained, all was at peace. When sin entered the world, it became disordered because everything was thrown off course. This is why the whole of creation groans and labors with birth pangs in expectation for the revealing of the sons of God (see Rom. 8:22).

God in His wisdom created mankind last. Isaiah lamented for Israel saying, "Who has measured the waters in the hollow of His hand, measured heaven with a span and calculated the dust of the earth in a measure? Weighed the mountains in scales and the hills in a balance? Who has directed the Spirit of the Lord, or as His counselor has taught Him?" (Is. 40:12-13) I imagine if God had created man first, man would have tried to tell God how, what, and when to create. Instead God created everything and then presented it to man. All he had to do was honor God and accept his place in the economy of God. Man had access to and dominion over everything in creation.

Obedience provides stability and keeps us in the will of God. Obedience also is our greatest expression of worship to God. When we obey Him, we acknowledge His sovereignty and ownership of all things. All of creation suffered when Adam and Eve disobeyed God. When we take matters into our own hands to try to help God, we are saying, in effect, that we should be His counselor or teacher.

All of our efforts to usurp God's authority lead to chaos and destruction. Restoration comes when we become responsible stewards over what God has given. If our lives are in disorder because of disobedience, only total submission to God will reverse our condition.

Often when we are overwhelmed by something, we try to take matters into our own hands. When Isaiah spoke of darkness and gross darkness covering the earth, he instructed us to arise and shine, to let the glory of God be seen in us. When we are reestablished in His righteousness, He will restore our place of dominion. The enemy always encourages us to take from the fruit of the tree of the knowledge of good and evil, to avoid God's authority and to take control of our own lives. If we could simply understand the power of obedience, we could draw from God's resources and provision. Solomon, a man of great wisdom, said that the whole matter of man is to fear God and keep His commandments (see Eccles. 12:13). The answer is not control—the answer is surrender.

The organized Church, like David, has risen from humble beginnings to now hold a place of prominence. She has become self-confident and self-reliant. She has set out many times to accomplish things for God, only to fall in ruins. Many moves of God ended in ash heaps of human effort. When the Bride marries the world system, she forsakes her Husband. Instead of relying on Him to provide for her, she sits upon the seven hills of human power and lives deliciously from the merchandise of the world (see Rev. 18). Many churches have set out to change the world, but have been swallowed up by it.

In the 1980's, many ministries that tried to do something for God fell under the sin of pride and lost everything that the Father had placed in their hands. The Charismatic Movement lost momentum because many people took what they had been given as an opportunity to set order to the world. Some squandered their gifts and talents in politics, others in business and entertainment; still others spent their resources finding fault with the rest of the church world. Each ministry resulted in death. Many ministries lay in ruins and millions of dollars have been lost in liquidation and bankruptcy.

Warfare of the Spirit

Today a particular thrust of the modern Church is spiritual warfare. In Matthew 26:52 Jesus said, "...for all who take the sword will perish by the sword." Many people have misunderstood spiritual warfare. God never called the Church to carnal warfare or warfare of the flesh. A person with a sword in hand most assuredly cannot build the Father's house. Second Corinthians 10:4 says, "For the weapons of our warfare are not carnal but mighty in God for pulling down strongholds." The enemy spends a lot of time trying to involve Christians in carnal warfare. He knows that when in the flesh, they'll lose their spiritual authority to destroy strongholds. When they quickly lose their rest, they become worn out and discouraged.

In spiritual warfare, all but one piece of armor God provides is defensive. According to Ephesians 6:14-17, this armor includes having your waist girded with truth, putting on the breastplate of righteousness, having your feet shod with the preparation of the gospel of peace, taking the shield of faith, and the helmet of salvation. When our obedience is made complete, He will avenge all disobedience (see 2 Cor. 10:5-6). We deal with the enemy by submitting to God. Our only offensive weapon is the sword of the Spirit, the Word of God. We do not have the right to bear any sword other than the sword of the Spirit. Any other sword does us more damage than good.

Jesus demonstrated this lesson when Peter cut off the ear of a soldier who had come to arrest Jesus in Gethsemane (see Lk. 22:49-51; Jn. 18:10-11). Jesus healed the man and illustrated that even in the most difficult situation, we must be obedient to the Word. Jesus said to bless those who curse you, do good to those who hate you, and pray for those who spitefully use and persecute you (see Mt. 5:44). Jesus healed the one who had come to take Him. We make our obedience complete by putting on the whole armor of God. If we follow God's principles, we experience victory.

The Greek word for sword in Ephesians 6:17 is not *logos,* or the written Word of God, but *rhema,* which is a quickened and living word. This is why Paul personally asked for prayer, that utterance might be given to him to boldly declare the mystery of the gospel (see Eph. 6:19). He knew that He had to speak an anointed gospel message to destroy the works of the enemy, one that came by prayer and supplication of a people committed to the warfare of the Spirit and not of the flesh.

The gospel is a mystery to the carnal mind. In First Corinthians 2:14 Paul writes, "But the natural man does not receive the things of the Spirit of God, for they are foolishness to him; nor can he know them, because they are spiritually discerned." The enemy has blinded the minds of unbelievers so they cannot receive the gospel. Only by prayer and the anointed word can these strongholds be broken. It is vital for the Church to return to God in prayer and commit to preaching the gospel to the world. As we begin to walk in the Spirit, we will begin to enter into His rest.

Our Choices Today

We in the Charismatic and Pentecostal Movements are at a crossroads today. We are in a position to choose the carnal way because we have found credibility with the world. We will either be swallowed up by the world or understand the perfect call of the Father to be in the world but not of it. At this juncture, it is important to walk in the Spirit. Our warfare has been accomplished and God is now calling for men of peace to build His house. Hebrews 4:9-10 says, "There remains therefore a rest for the people of God. For he who has entered His rest has himself also ceased from his works...." Many cannot enter in because of their lack of faith or disobedience. Today, if we will hear His voice and not harden our hearts, we will enter into His rest. Put your faith in God and totally depend upon His resources, His abilities, and ultimately, His control. Be diligent to enter into that rest.

Finally, we need to recognize this appointed time in history. Just as Solomon was appointed to build the temple of God's glory and David had already set aside most of the provision needed, we must simply build as God directs. We can observe through Church history that most of the warfare has already been accomplished. The precious truths that are so easily accepted today did not come cheaply. Early pioneers of the faith paid dearly for them.

In the beginning of the Pentecostal Movement, those who dared to speak in tongues were forced to leave their churches and were ostracized by the greater Body of Christ. The Latter Rain, Charismatic, and Jesus People Movements embraced truth (i.e., prophecy, ministry gifts, worship and praise, fivefold ministry, etc.) and many suffered great personal loss, even their ministries. Today, most of the truths introduced by these movements have become widely accepted.

We must lay down our carnal warfare and receive the Kingdom. This Kingdom can only be inherited and received. Just as David secured the victory for Solomon, Jesus Christ has secured it for the Church. Sons need to receive the Kingdom that the Father has prepared.

As Jesus faced great persecution from the religious leaders of His day, He made a statement that has been misinterpreted and misused ever since. In Matthew 11:12, Jesus said, "And from the days of John the Baptist until now the kingdom of heaven suffers violence, and the violent take it by force." I've heard the second part of this verse quoted many times, but the first portion is disregarded. Jesus said from the days of John the Baptist *until now*, His ministry would be different. From this point on, Jesus would simply speak the word and live the message before the people. Jesus is not a Man of violence, but a Man of rest.

Had Jesus chosen to take the Kingdom by force, He certainly would not have entered into Jerusalem on a colt. Even His closest followers did not understand how this strategy could work. Jesus demonstrated that when He was obedient even unto death, nothing was withheld from Him. When His obedience was fulfilled, all power was given to Him. Jesus now sits on the right hand of power on High until all of His enemies are made His footstool (see Heb. 10:12-13). The Church needs to follow that same pattern in order to sit with Him in heavenly places (Eph. 2:6). We are His Body, the fullness of Him who fills all in all and the Father will put all things under our feet. It is time for the Church to ascend to that place of rest in God, sitting in heavenly places far above all principalities and power, not being tempted to fight our battles, but placing our confidence totally in God.

All the materials for the house have been gathered by our forefathers. The price has already been paid for our faith. Now is the time to possess the inheritance prepared for us. It's time to build the Father's house.

Chapter 13

A House
of Restoration

Although David was forbidden to build a house for God, God expressed His love for David by extending His mercy to David's seed. God promised;

And it shall be, when your days are fulfilled, when you must go to be with your fathers, that I will set up your seed after you, who will be of your sons; and I will establish his kingdom. He shall build Me a house, and I will establish his throne forever. I will be his Father, and he shall be My son; and I will not take My mercy away from him, as I took it from him who was before you (1 Chronicles 17:11-14).

This particular covenant that God established with David is referred to as the sure mercies of David.

Jesus Christ, the Son of David, came to seek and to save that which was lost (see Lk. 19:10). The promise of God to the wandering and sick sheep was to raise up His servant David to be a shepherd over them (see Ezek. 34). Shepherds must have an understanding of the sure mercies of David to fulfill the Davidic ministry God is raising up. Jesus said when someone is in the Father's hands, no one can pluck him out (see Jn. 10:29). This is a place of security. The Father not only draws us to the saving power of Christ; He also secures us in His hands. This was the promise to David. God, Himself, would be a Father to David's seed.

Further application of the covenant of the sure mercies of David is found in Second Samuel 7:14-15. "I will be his Father, and he shall be My son. If he commits iniquity, I will chasten him with the rod of men and with the blows of the sons of men. But My mercy shall not depart from him, as I took it from Saul, whom I removed from before you." As a part of this covenant of mercy, God also promised to discipline with His own hand. Thus the Father desires to keep us, but also to make us into the people He wants us to be. His mercy is a firm commitment to actively participate in our lives. The Father's role is to develop the nature of His children, not just nurture them.

I expect to see a tremendous ingathering of people to include not only the harvest of new souls, but also the restoration of the wandering and stray sheep. In order to see and be a part of this ingathering, we must recognize the principles of restoration revealed through the sure mercies of David.

Restoring the Lost Sheep

Before the gospel was presented to the Gentiles, Jesus came to His own: the lost sheep of the house of Israel. His ministry was one of restoration as well as one of reconciliation. The people Jesus most often associated with were considered castaways by the religious leaders. We cannot be like these religious leaders or we will miss the move of God altogether. Jesus came unto His own and they did not receive Him, but as many as received Him, He gave power to become the sons of God (see Jn. 1:11-12).

Jesus used three illustrations in Luke 15 to demonstrate our responsibilities to the lost ones who belong to God. He began the parable with the story of the lost sheep, continued with the lost coin, and ended with the prodigal son. Each story tells about something that was lost and later found, followed by a time of great rejoicing.

In the first illustration, Jesus said, "What man of you, having a hundred sheep, if he loses one of them, does not leave the ninety-nine in the wilderness, and go after the one which is lost until he finds it?" (Lk. 15:4) God knows where the wandering sheep are because He loves them. Sheep are simpleminded and gentle animals, so they are easily led but scatter at any sign of danger. It is the shepherd's responsibility to make sure nothing harms the sheep. If they have wandered off, the shepherd must look for them and return them to the flock because sheep cannot find their way back.

I have talked to many people who left their previous churches to come to Mt. Zion Temple and no one ever called to see about them. We must realize the importance of going after wandering sheep and assume the responsibility for finding out what made them run. When the lost are found, there is reason to rejoice and celebrate. Shepherds of God must know the Father greatly loves the lost sheep of the house of Israel. Many churches spend time evangelizing, strongly encouraging their members to bring new people to church, yet they do not have a heart for their own lost sheep.

At one point in my ministry, I began complaining to God about some people who were taking up all of my time with their problems. It seemed like I didn't have time for anyone else. The Lord reminded me that a shepherd is called to the lost sheep of the house. God said, "If you will commit yourself to the lost sheep, I will take care of the 99; out of the 99, I will raise up workers to labor in the harvest." If we, as shepherds, will make it our responsibility to attend to the lost sheep, we will see the Lord of the harvest supply laborers and we'll reap in abundance from His harvest fields.

This word changed my whole perspective about the church. The majority of people or the 99 who attend an assembly do not need greater oversight than the preaching of the Word and a place to worship. From

time to time they may need help or counsel, but as a
rule they just don't need much personal pastoral care.
On the other hand, those who are the weaker vessels,
those more susceptible to disease and danger, require
closer constant attention. Most shepherds, especially
those who want to build large churches, spend most of
their time attending to the people they consider
productive members of the flock, believing they will
contribute a lot to the church. Yet, God will not bless a
shepherd who does not have a true shepherd's heart.
He is raising up shepherds who will feed the flock, bind
up the broken ones, and strengthen the sick.

It is hard to understand why God allows His sheep
to stay with a shepherd who will not tend them. He
promises to be a Shepherd to His people and to raise up
shepherds who will have a heart for the sheep. In this
day, we are seeing a great ingathering as the Great
Shepherd fulfills His promise to gather the scattered
sheep from the four corners of the earth. God will lead
them to a safe place where they will be well tended and
gladly received. This seeking of the lost sheep demonstrates the work of Jesus Christ, the true Shepherd.
Jesus said in John 10:1-4:

> *...he who does not enter the sheepfold by the door,*
> *but climbs up some other way, the same is a thief*
> *and a robber. But he who enters by the door is the*
> *shepherd of the sheep. ...the sheep hear his voice;*
> *and he calls his own sheep by name and leads*
> *them out. ...the sheep follow him, for they know*
> *his voice* (John 10:1-4).

Jesus came in the door of the sheepfold to reach His flock. Our Shepherd came seeking the lost.

Finding Those Lost in the House

The second illustration speaks about a lost coin. Jesus related a story about a woman who had ten coins but had lost one. Will she not light a lamp, sweep the house, and seek diligently until she finds it? (see Luke 15:8-9.) It is interesting to note that the coin was lost in the house. At Mt. Zion Temple, we have seen many people restored who were lost even while they remained in their churches. In fact, many of them had been wounded in the house of their friends. The sad part is, nobody noticed. It is our responsibility to find them and restore them to God. Here, the woman was responsible for losing the coin. She had neglected to keep it in a safe place. She sought for it with urgency because she knew she was responsible. There are multitudes of people who are lost in the house. We need to seek them out so they can be restored to their rightful places.

The worth of many people in the Father's house goes unrecognized. They never receive restoration because many shepherds believe these people are more bother than worth. They are never asked to do anything in the church because their shepherd does not see them as God does. When Jesus came to earth, He approached people others wouldn't have anything to do with because He knew their hearts. A good example is the Samaritan woman at the well (see Jn. 4). Not only was she discriminated against by the Jews because of her race, but she was also a woman who had a bad reputation. Why did Jesus pay her any mind? He loved her, yes, but He also saw something in her no one else did.

When He shared the gospel with her and prophesied about her life, she returned and evangelized her entire community. She became a source of life to those who would not associate with her. If we could see as God sees and take on His character, we would see a great harvest. We need to ask ourselves whether or not we will receive the kinds of people the Father wants to send. Would we be open to accept their gifts?

The woman who lost the coin represents the Church, or the Bride of Christ. When Jesus ascended, He gave gifts to men (see Eph. 4:8). These gifts are distributed as He wills, by the Holy Spirit (see 1 Cor. 12:11). Everything the Church needs for the edifying of herself is within the many-membered Body of Christ. Since we are responsible for the lost, we must be like that woman who carefully tends to the needs of others through the gifts of the Holy Spirit. We must recognize as well that our needs may be met by the gift of someone we least expect to meet them. Many are sick and even die prematurely because they do not discern the Lord's body (see 1 Cor. 11:29-30). When the Church assumes responsibility for those who are lost, she will begin to find and restore them. Only then can the Body be healthy and whole.

The Return of Sons

The last illustration, the parable of the prodigal son, tells how the lost son left the house (see Lk. 15:11-32).

He wanted to use his inheritance for his own purposes. After he had wasted all that he had, he realized his only hope was to return to his father's house. He didn't think he would be received as a son. But because he had nowhere else to turn, he would have been satisfied being a servant in his father's house. However, when he returned home, his father greeted him with open arms. Although he had wasted his inheritance, he did not lose sonship—he was still a son.

Since the prodigal son left his father's house on his own accord, it had to be his choice to return. He who willfully leaves God's house cannot come back by the urging of another person. Like the prodigal, he must *come to himself* and realize his only hope is in Father's house. This change of heart requires the dynamic work of the Father. When someone is in the Father's hand, no man can pluck him out (see Jn. 10:29). Perhaps only the Father can understand the prodigals. He never quits loving them and always anticipates their return.

The prodigal sons who return to the house will know that they don't deserve anything. They know that they have been given their share and wasted it. Although they are prepared to be servants, the Father will declare them to be sons. Romans 8:19 tells us that the whole of creation eagerly waits for the revealing of the sons of God in the earth. The restored prodigal son still had access to all that was his father's. He was given a ring, a robe, and shoes for his feet. He knew that he didn't deserve these things, for he had spent all that was his. The prodigals who experience restoration in the house will reveal and manifest the glory and power of God. They who are dead will be alive again. They will know where their help came from and will fully understand the restoring love of the Father.

This pattern is demonstrated in the lives of the disciples. When Jesus started His ministry, He gathered a group of proud, self-centered individuals. Their immaturity was revealed by their actions. When Jesus was arrested and crucified, they fled their responsibilities as the called of God. They who thought they could accomplish the most for God, fell the furthest and hit the hardest. It was not until they had experienced Pentecost that their captivity was turned.

Peter, who had denied the Lord three times, preached on the Day of Pentecost and 3,000 were saved (see Acts 2). In John 21, Jesus asked Peter three different times if he loved Him. Each time Peter responded, the Lord commissioned him to feed or tend His sheep. He rose out of failure to manifest a life totally committed to Christ. He was willing to lay down his life because he had experienced the power of resurrection. Multitudes of prodigals are *coming to themselves*, realizing who they are, and knowing where their hope lies. When they come back to the house, we must have the heart of the Father to receive them.

Receiving the Captives and Their Gifts

The Book of Zechariah is a record of the restoration of the temple and its story parallels what God is doing today. The children of Israel were being regathered following their captivity in Babylon to rebuild the temple in Jerusalem. Today, God is calling His children out of

Babylon (or the world) and bringing them to His temple or holy city that He is rebuilding.

God told the leaders to receive the captives and their gifts when they came. Zechariah 6:10 says, "Receive the gift from the captives—from Heldai, Tobijah, and Jedaiah, who have come from Babylon— and go the same day and enter the house of Josiah the son of Zephaniah." These particular names hold great significance: *Heldai* means worldliness; *Tobijah* means the goodness of Jehovah; *Jedaiah* means "Jehovah has known." These captives are to be brought to *Josiah*, which means "founded of Jehovah." The captives of Babylon are brought to the house that the Lord Himself has built. *Jedaiah* represents those brought back by the Lord. They are prodigals returning home. *Tobijah* represents those who have been overlooked; nobody sees their real worth but God. It is because of His goodness or mercy that they are reached like the lost coins that must be found and restored. *Heldai* represents those who have strayed after the things of the world. Because of His love, the Father seeks and returns them to His house like the lost sheep.

God commanded that when the captives come, we are to receive their silver and gold for the rebuilding of the temple. The elder son was not able to receive the captive (the prodigal son) or anything he had to offer when he returned to his father's house.

Gold represents the work of God in the life of the believer. When the captives return, they will have gold worked in them by God. They will realize that God has never left them or stopped working in their lives. The time they spent outside the Father's house will be turned into a mature and fruitful time. Because of the Father's mercy, they will return with gold.

When gold is processed, all impurities and dross are melted. During the process of purification, the dross comes to the surface. If the Church only sees the dross and not the gold, she will not be able to receive the gifts from the captives when they return. Elder sons must pray for their eyes to be opened to see the gold.

The Babylonians captured the children of Israel, destroyed the temple, and took the treasures of it. When it was time to rebuild the temple, God prepared a way to have the gold returned to His house. When God delivers His people, He delivers them with abundance. The children of Israel did not leave Egypt empty-handed. When the Lord turns the captivity of His people in this day, they will not come back empty-handed either. They will come with gold and we are commanded of God to receive them when they come.

When the Lord promised that He would give me the treasures of darkness, the hidden riches of secret places, and that I would know the Lord who called me by name, I first thought He was speaking about finances. I realize now that those hidden treasures, mentioned in Isaiah 45, refer to the treasures stored in the vaults of Babylon at the time of the Israeli captivity. That passage was a prophecy concerning King Cyrus who would be raised up by God to restore the treasures of the Lord's house to the children of Israel when they returned to Jerusalem. Spiritually, it refers to the captives of the world system that God is calling back into His house. They themselves are a partial fulfillment of the prophecy of the hidden treasures because their gifts were hidden, but are now being brought to light.

If we are obedient to the Father's call in this day, we will indeed see an abundant financial increase. Many ministries in the Body of Christ have failed because of their unhealthy and unrighteous pursuit of money. Psalm 37:25 plainly declares that we should never see the righteous forsaken or his descendants begging for bread, yet we have watched television ministers beg shamelessly and relentlessly for money. Flesh works are kept alive with flesh works, but that which the Father builds, He will finance. Jehovah-Jirah, the Lord who provides, reveals Himself only to those who open their eyes to see His work in this time of harvest.

An Example of Restoration

The ingathering has already begun. As an example, a few years ago I met with a young couple, David and Debra, in my office late at night. It was an emergency situation, and they agreed to meet with me. They had two small children but were ready to end their marriage.

David had been raised in a legalistic church and had been a missionary to South America. When he returned from the mission field, he and Debra were married and he became the youth pastor of his home church. Along with personal problems, David was confused and had struggled in his spiritual walk because of the legalism and hypocrisy that he had witnessed in his church. His relationship with God did not prepare him for what he had to face, so he left the church for the pleasures of the world. Since he had always been taught that his was the only true church, he felt he couldn't go anywhere else.

After eight years, the Lord mercifully began softening his heart. The Lord told him to come to Mt. Zion Temple. He sat in my office wanting to know if he could ever minister again if he divorced. God had been dealing with his wife as well, but reconciliation seemed impossible. As I listened, I knew that their only hope was God. They needed a miracle. I suggested that we pray.

The Lord gave me a word of prophecy for them. When a prophecy is given for someone, the secrets of the heart will be manifest and the person will fall on his face and worship God in truth. The word that the Lord gave me for David was that God had been with him all along the way. It grieved the Father to allow him to go through the hard places and that He had to turn His face. It would be through these things that God would deal with his heart and make him into the person the Father wanted him to be. When Jesus was on the cross, the Father turned His face away, but the purpose of God was accomplished through the great pain and suffering.

That night the Lord broke strongholds; restoration began to work in their hearts. There were many other things that David and Debra had to deal with in the months to follow, but God did a complete work of restoration. God worked to change their hearts and their marriage was restored.

A few years later, the Lord told me that He wanted to restore ministry to David. When I told him, the word of the Lord began to change his heart. His circumstances began to change as well. Their finances had been in terrible shape. Eight years of riotous living had taken everything. They had no plan or purpose for the future. Financial planning was not a priority. When David surrendered his life totally to God for full-time service, he was offered a buy-out from one of the big three car companies. He received a substantial amount of money that more than compensated for the equity he would have built up had he been a wise steward during those eight lost years. The Father's restoration was complete and had been accomplished in abundance.

When the ministry of restoration fully takes effect, it will be one of the most exciting times in history. There is nothing like the joy that comes when you find something that has been lost; but those who were lost will have an even greater rejoicing. Psalm 126 says it best:

When the Lord brought back the captivity of Zion, we were like those who dream. Then our mouth was filled with laughter, and our tongue with singing. Then they said among the nations, "The Lord has done great things for them." The Lord has done great things for us, and we are glad. Bring back our captivity, O Lord, as the streams in the South. Those who sow in tears shall reap in joy. He who continually goes forth weeping, bearing seed for sowing, shall doubtless come again

with rejoicing, bringing his sheaves with him
(Psalm 126).

The Church has tried to walk in full sonship and
failed. Sons in the house have used the gifts of the
Father for selfish purposes, just like the prodigal son
did. Through the years, many people have become discouraged and left the Church. Others have stayed in
the house but are dying there. The wind of God is blow-
ing today; we will see a great resurrection, as
prophesied by Ezekiel (see Exek. 37). The dry bones
will live! Many people will be brought back to life by
God and will return with a greater understanding of
the Word of God. Like the prodigal son, they will return
wanting only to serve, but the Father will restore them
as full-heir sons.

Chapter 14

Restoration of the House

God is not only restoring individuals, He also is restoring His house. This is referred to in the Scriptures as the restoration of David's tabernacle. Amos 9:11-15 speaks about a time when God will rebuild the tabernacle of David; God will repair the damages and raise it up from ruins. Restoration will bring in an unprecedented harvest and when it is complete, God says that He will plant His people and they shall never again be pulled up. The Father's house is a house of planting and be assured that it is also a house of security. Jesus said that when we are in the Father's hand, no one can pluck us out of us (see Jn. 10:29). We can rest knowing that we will be firmly planted in Father's house.

The tabernacle of David was unlike the temple built by Solomon because God did not allow David to build a permanent structure. David pitched a tent that was used to temporarily house the ark of the covenant, the presence of God, until a permanent temple was constructed. Amos was referring to this tabernacle, but he was not speaking of a physical building. God's concern is with the issues of the heart, not the works of man's hands. Today many people are expecting the literal rebuilding of the temple in Israel, but I encourage you to focus on the spiritual rebuilding of God's house.

David's Tabernacle as a Type in Acts

In Acts 15, the Bible speaks about David's tabernacle being restored during the time of the apostles. This chapter tells that a church council had been assembled to discuss particular issues regarding the Gentile church started by Paul and Barnabas. Messengers from the church in Jerusalem had come to Antioch because they believed that Jewish law should be followed by the Gentile believers. Paul and Barnabas disagreed with them, so the issue was brought before the Jerusalem church council.

After long debate, James, the head of the church, made a judgment based upon the Scriptures and the knowledge that God was obviously moving in their midst. He said that the Gentile church was the fulfillment of Amos' prophecy; God would draw from every nation a people called by His name and they would not be required to follow Jewish laws and traditions. God wanted to restore the tabernacle of David.

The restoration would open the door for all people to seek the Lord, and He would change and direct them.

The order of the tabernacle of David followed this direction. It did not resemble the tabernacle of Moses, which was divided into distinct areas that separated the people from God's presence. The tabernacle of David offered immediate access to the presence of God. Although both tabernacles had an order of praise, David's offering to God was always spontaneous and from the heart.

David's tabernacle is a type of what God desires in His Church. Religious systems build barriers to keep people away from God, but the tabernacle of David allows people access to the presence of God. Dwelling in God's presence will change hearts and produce joy.

The Jerusalem council decided that they must first introduce the people to God and then let Him perform a work of righteousness in them. Righteousness changes an individual on the inside and manifests itself in his life style. This concept is different from legalism, which seeks to impose righteousness by adherence to strict laws—outward actions. When we realize that God's plan for today is true righteousness, we will experience the greatest harvest of all time. It will be a time of unspeakable joy, full of glory. Joy will be the strength of the people, bringing them to a place of holiness and purity in heart.

David's Tabernacle as a Type in Revelation

John saw David's tabernacle in his revelation as it descended out of Heaven. "And I heard a loud voice from heaven saying, 'Behold, the tabernacle of God is with men...' " (Rev. 21:3). The dwelling place of God, the presence of God, would be in the midst of His people. Revelation 21:22 says, "But I saw no temple in it, for the Lord God Almighty and the Lamb are its temple." God's desire has always been to live with His people. God told David that His presence would abide in a tabernacle. A temple is glorious because of its structure; a tent or tabernacle is glorious because of the presence inside. God puts His treasure in earthen vessels so any glory would be His. This not only applies to the corporate Church, but also to each of us individually.

Jesus said, "In My Father's house are many mansions..." (Jn. 14:2). God has prepared mansions for His house. We are those mansions or abiding places in the earth. Revelation 21:18-21 lists the precious stones used for the walls, foundations, gates, and streets. Isaiah prophesied that these precious stones are what God will use to restore those who are afflicted, tossed with tempest, and not comforted. Those people are precious in His house because of His kindness and mercy toward them (see Is. 54:11-12). Isaiah continued, "All your children shall be taught by the Lord, and great shall be the peace of your children" (Is. 54:13). Jesus referred to this in John 6:44 by explaining, "No one can come to Me unless the Father who sent Me draws him...." The Father's house is filled with children of His choosing, those who have heard the Father's voice and come to Him. Corporately, we are the glorious tabernacle of God.

The Stream of God's Presence

There is a throne of authority in the house of David that God has established and will cause to abide forever. Revelation 22:1-2 says that John saw "a pure river of water of life, clear as crystal, proceeding from the throne of God and of the Lamb. ...on either side of the river, was the tree of life. ...The leaves of the tree were for the healing of the nations." David had an intimate knowledge of this river and its origin. He understood that the power entrusted to him proceeded from the flow of God's presence.

David said in Psalm 46:4-5, "There is a river whose streams shall make glad the city of God, the holy place of the tabernacle of the Most High. God is in the midst of her, she shall not be moved...." This stream or river of God's divine presence is very significant to the tabernacle of David. David loved this river. His intimacy with God produced great authority in his life. David danced before the Lord when the ark of the covenant was returned because He knew Israel's victories had only come because of the ark of God's presence in their midst (see 2 Sam. 6). He demonstrated his love for the presence of God by establishing an elaborate order of praise in the tabernacle. He hired professional singers and musicians to continually praise during the day and throughout the night (see 1 Chron. 9:33). The tabernacle of David truly displayed the love he had for the presence of God.

Many people have not understood the power of this tabernacle and have assumed that the restoration of

David's tabernacle means a restoration of praise and worship in the Church. They have greatly erred by overlooking the great power residing in the tabernacle. Praise and worship are consequences rather than causes of the presence of God.

Many people receive only a partial or temporary restoration. Some have a very superficial spiritual life because they believe they can invoke the presence of God with ritualistic worship or praise. Jeremiah warned the teachers of his day that God would judge them because they had healed the hurt of the people only slightly. Jeremiah 8:22 says, "Is there no balm in Gilead, is there no physician there? Why then is there no recovery for the health of the daughter of my people?" The answer is clear. We are a people who prefer to cover or treat the effects and symptoms of a problem rather than examine its causes.

The essence of David's tabernacle was not worship and praise. Worship was the result of the people entering into God's presence. In many churches today, praise, not God, has become the focus of the service. Praise and worship are expressions of love that come forth as we plunge into the presence of God. The expressions are varied in demonstration, but all true praise begins in the river and flows out of us.

God Is Our Focus

In the restoration of David's tabernacle, the Church will acknowledge that anything genuine and lasting in the Father's house proceeds from Him. All that proceeds from man is temporary and superficial. Only that which proceeds from God is eternal. The restoration of David's tabernacle will be complete when we fix our eyes on God.

Every time there has been a great move of God, man began to question the particular reason God visited him. After supposing the reason for the blessings, people began marketing their brand of Christianity to the Body of Christ, attributing success to the order of doctrine they created. It is very difficult for many people to move with God because the structures that man builds are not movable. This is why God prefers to dwell in tents; He's always moving.

Whenever another move of God begins, people whose focus has switched to man-made order are not willing to make the change and so resist the new move. God wants His order to be established, not ours. New wine does not last in old wineskins; we must be flexible in order to flow with God.

In the Charismatic Movement, a definite order of praise and worship has emerged. Many churches have built a doctrine called "Restoration of David's Tabernacle," supposing this order to be similar to David's. Pentecostals did not accept Charismatic order because they believed their own order of service was directly given by God. Their order could be traced back to the Jerusalem council. Throughout Church history, people have believed that their particular pattern was correct because they had witnessed God in its inception. The fact is, God does not permanently set any form or order. God knows man will eventually worship the order rather than Him. Therefore, God changes the order to keep our focus on Him. If God had meant a form to be permanent, David certainly would not have been inspired to change the form set by Moses.

In the great move we are now entering, we must remember that the order is not the important focus— God is. With this understanding, we can reach out to the universal Body of Christ and allow all tribes and tongues to worship God in their own order. Recently, in the Charismatic stream, there has been a renewed interest in liturgical worship. Men are trying to reinstate church rituals in an attempt to capture former glory. Although God can use old forms for His glory, He does not set a mandate to return to them.

True Worship

When Jesus met the woman at Jacob's well, He spoke to her and revealed the secrets of her heart. This was true prophetic ministry. When a prophet reveals the secrets of men's hearts, the people fall on their faces and worship God. Prophetic ministry leads the way to true worship. After her heart was exposed, she said to Jesus, "Sir, I perceive that You are a prophet" (Jn. 4:19). Then she spoke about the differences between the Jews and the Samaritans in worship. The Samaritans worshiped on the mountain and the Jews worshiped in Jerusalem. Order, rather than God, was her focus. Jesus said to her in John 4:22-23, "You worship what you do not know.... . But the hour is coming, and now is, when the true worshipers will worship the Father in spirit and truth; for the Father is seeking such to worship Him."

The river or fountain of God is the only true source of all that is real and vital. Only with an honest heart and by the prompting of the Holy Spirit can we produce acceptable praise to God. True or sincere worship begins with an open heart before God. Proverbs 4:23 says, "Keep your heart with all diligence, for out of it spring the issues of life." David worshiped in truth because his praise proceeded from his heart in response to the presence of God. David's worship was of the Spirit, the wellspring of life.

Spontaneous response to God is another important observation regarding David's tabernacle. David easily responded to the presence of God. Spontaneous response will cause the river of God to flow to other people. This is why true worship is the key to soul winning, or to any other work that God wants to perform through the Church.

After the Samaritan woman talked to Jesus, she left her waterpot and returned to the city to tell people about Jesus. When anyone drinks from the water Jesus gives, they will lay down their old waterpots in exchange for the fountain of everlasting life. Revival stems from true worship. However, if we lose sight of our focus, we will not be fruitful.

True worship comes from a person who has known and experienced the true mercies of God, or as the Bible terms it, the sure mercies of David. The woman at the well was accepted by someone who knew everything about her. Jesus reached beyond racial prejudice by speaking to a Samaritan; beyond social prejudice by speaking to a woman with a bad reputation; and beyond religious prejudice because of their differences in worship order. Jesus reached out in love and mercy to someone who was scarred by a great stigma of rejection to offer her the fountain of life. God isn't concerned about what we can do for Him, but what He can do for us. This is the revelation of a merciful God.

God's Prerogative to Choose

Rome was the world's greatest power during the writing of the Roman epistle, and the church there wanted to be the center or focus of religion. The Roman church needed understanding about the power of God's choosing. The word written to them was, "...that the purpose of God according to election might stand, not of works but of Him who calls" (Rom. 9:11). God does the choosing, not man. In Romans 9 Paul speaks about God loving Jacob and hating Esau. He says that God preferred Jacob over Esau before either was born. Neither had done anything to deserve God's favor or disfavor. God simply chose Jacob, not Esau; thus it was not Jacob's merit that qualified him to be used in the Kingdom of God.

This truth is foreign to our thinking. Our logical minds don't seem to be able to comprehend that God simply makes choices. The Word declares that God's thoughts and ways are higher than ours, as far as the heavens are from the earth (see Is. 55:8-9). Jesus said that no man can come to Him unless the Father draws him (see Jn. 6:44). This is not only hard to understand, it is offensive to us because we would like to be able to take pride in our salvation. Paul reports that God told Moses, "...I will have mercy on whomever I will have mercy, and I will have compassion on whomever I will have compassion. So then it is not of him who wills, nor of him who runs, but of God who shows mercy" (Rom. 9:15-16). The whole focus is on God, the rightful center of true worship.

Our Source

In John's revelation, all of Heaven focused on Him who was the source of all things. This is why the 24 elders, who sit around the throne, throw their crowns at the feet of Him who sits on the throne. In Heaven, they know that He is the source.

If we cannot understand that in Him, by Him, and through Him everything exists (see Jn. 1:3), we cannot offer a sacrifice in the tabernacle that is pleasing to God. He is looking for an offering of Spirit, not of flesh. He will only accept an offering of faith, not of human effort. If you believe you can offer just anything to God, it will be like Cain's sacrifice—unacceptable. David's greatest experience of worship took place after he sinned with Bathsheba, for it was predicated upon his absolute need for God. The word *worship* means to kneel or prostrate oneself. It is not just the action of laying flat or prostrate; it is utter surrender to God.

David, in his prayer of repentance, said, "Behold, You desire truth in the inward parts, and in the hidden part You will make me to know wisdom" (Ps. 51:6). When David had a revelation of himself, a person brought forth in iniquity and conceived in sin, it brought him liberty because he knew his relationship with God was wholly dependent on God's mercy. Jesus said in John 8:32, "And you shall know the truth and the truth shall make you free." Second Corinthians 3:17 says, "...and where the Spirit of the Lord is, there is liberty." Truth brings freedom and the Spirit brings liberty. In David's tabernacle, liberty is more than the freedom to express ourselves. It is exoneration or freedom from the burden of sin and death. The spirit of truth gives us the freedom to become everything that Jesus has called us to be.

A new dimension of praise and worship is coming to the Church. In the past, Christians have emphasized praise and worship so His presence would come, but I'm looking for that which is initiated by God, not man. This will require us to wait upon the Lord, and it is hard to wait without doing anything. In Revelation 8:1, when the seventh seal was opened (as the revelation of John came forth), there was a silence in Heaven. It was a time of waiting upon God. When Habakkuk waited on God for delivering power, he said, "But the Lord is in His holy temple. Let all the earth keep silence before Him" (Hab. 2:20).

Habakkuk lived in a time much like ours, when the earth was filled with violence, iniquity, and injustice. Habakkuk cried out to God because judgment or punishment was not visited upon the evildoers. Yet when God revealed His plan, Habakkuk complained. God could never show us His complete divine plan because we are just too ignorant to comprehend it. Only God can intervene and improve the condition of the world. Man has tried without success. It's time for us to keep silent and know that God is in His holy temple; He will come and do His work.

The River of Life

The healing of the nations will come from the river that proceeds from the throne of God. Ezekiel also saw the power of the river. In chapter 47, he said that wherever the river went, there was healing and resurrection life. The river would also bring a very great multitude of fish, or a harvest of souls. Along the banks of the river would grow all kinds of trees and their fruit would be food and their leaves medicine. This is everything that God wants the Church to be.

The work of God our Father is to bring fruitfulness to the Church through chastening and pruning, to bring resurrection life to prodigal sons, and to bring about a time of great rejoicing and celebration in His presence. We can expect to see these things in the midst of the great harvest.

Since it is the river that provides the healing of the nations, we must tell others about the river. Wherever the river goes, there is life. Therefore, wherever we go, we must bring life and healing. When we as the corporate Church begin to see the power of the river, we will change our judgmental attitudes. We will do everything possible to make the river available to everyone; just as Jesus took the river to the lame man who waited at the pool of Bethesda, we will take it to the lost who cannot come on their own (see Jn. 5:1-9).

When the Lord began to show me the river, I immediately made changes in our church program. I shortened the length of our new members' class from 32 to 16 weeks. Newcomers would still establish the foundational teaching of Christ in their lives, but have a faster entry into the church. The most significant change was in my attitude as I began teaching that we cannot produce righteousness in the lives of people; only God can do that. Our responsibility is to offer Christ to people and trust that God will begin a work of righteousness in them. Our obedience immediately resulted in explosive growth. Over just a few years, our attendance tripled. Hundreds of people were added to our church. Because of our change in attitude, God was able to impart a sense of community much stronger than we ever could have done. We began introducing people to God, not to our religion.

The Church has often tried to hold forth the religion of man instead of the word of life as Philippians 2:16 exhorts us to do. God moves in great awakenings and revivals, bringing tremendous harvest, but man tries to control the move. Even with the best intentions, the result is a man-made structure that cannot offer salvation or transform lives.

Just as the Jerusalem council had to reevaluate what was required of believers, we cannot put requirements on people that God does not. We must remove any barriers that we have built because Jesus said in Matthew 11:30, "For My yoke is easy and My burden is light."

The scribes and Pharisees tried to shut everyone out of the kingdom of heaven. Jesus lamented, "...for you neither go in yourselves, nor do you allow those who are entering to go in" (Mt. 23:13). We must open wide the gates and indeed declare aloud, "Whoever will, let him come and drink from the fountain flowing in the Father's house!" The Father's house is the restoration of David's tabernacle in the earth. We must know how to relate to the world and to each other as we are called to be ministers of reconciliation like Jesus. We will be those who build the old waste places and raise up the foundations of many generations; and we will be called repairers of the breach, the restorers of streets to dwell in (see Is. 58:12).

In the midst of tremendous need and the overwhelming problems of our day, there is a solution: the river that proceeds from the throne of God. Only when we acknowledge this, can we evangelize the lost. Know that in your innermost being is the Holy Spirit, the resource or river that will bring life to them. He who has ears to hear, let him hear what the Spirit is speaking to the Church. Revelation 22:17 says, "And the Spirit and the bride say, 'Come!' And let him who hears say, 'Come!' And let him who thirsts come. And whoever desires, let him take of the water of life freely."

Chapter 15

The Secret Place in the House

In the great visitation of this day, our relationship with the Father in the secret place holds the most significance. As Jesus spoke to His disciples about the scribes' and Pharisees' outward observance of religion, He said that they may appear righteous to men, but inside they are full of hypocrisy and lawlessness (Mt. 23:28).

Jesus, on the other hand, did not appear very religious outwardly, yet He demonstrated great authority from God. In Matthew 6:17-18, Jesus also said, "But you, when you fast, anoint your head and wash you face, so that you do not appear to men to be fasting, but to your Father who is in the secret place;

and your Father who sees in secret will reward you openly."

Only in the secret place can we develop an intimate relationship with God. The Father and son relationship is our individual quest in God. When we mature in intimate relationship as sons, the Church as a whole will be complete in Christ as His Bride. The Word declares that in the final days of time, the Son will Himself be fully submitted to the Father that God may be all in all (see 1 Cor. 15:28). Where will we find the Father? He dwells in the secret place.

Dwelling in the Secret Place

The secret place represents our personal or intimate relationship with God. When we first come to God, we receive salvation in the Son and are commanded to speak and to share the good news. When we receive the baptism of the Holy Spirit, we are equipped to demonstrate or manifest God's power. However, in the secret place with the Father, we are called to a closer relationship with Him.

In the secret place, God is not concerned about what we say or do, but who we are. His focus is our hearts. He dwells in the secret place of our hearts and will reveal what is there.

The scribes and Pharisees did not dwell with God in the secret place. They did not have a relationship with Him. That is the reason they lacked fruit. Fullness or fruitfulness will only come through the abiding work of the Father. Jesus said, "I am the true vine, and My

Father is the vinedresser. Every branch in Me that does not bear fruit He takes away; and every branch that bears fruit He prunes, that it may bear more fruit" (Jn. 15:1-2). The Father is the judge and He is responsible for the harvest.

Jesus also said that there is nothing covered that will not be revealed, or hidden that will not be known (see Lk. 12:2). The Father will ultimately reveal what is in the secret places of men's hearts, good or bad. We need a secret abiding place in the presence of the Father so He can reveal our hearts to this generation. Being found in the secret place is very important if we are to stand in the day of judgment.

Power in the Secret Place

The Church's greatest power comes from her secret-place relationship with God. Psalm 91:1 says, "He who dwells in the secret place of the Most High shall abide under the shadow of the Almighty." Verse 7 continues, "A thousand may fall at your side, and ten thousand at your right hand; but it shall not come near you." God has set His love upon us; therefore, He will deliver us and set us on high, because we have known His name (see Ps. 91:14). The needs of the world will be met by a people who have a secret-place relationship with God, a people who will call upon the Lord and hear Him answer. Because David had this type of relationship with God, he was prepared to face any conflict that arose, even a Philistine giant.

Many people begin their walk with God with a sincere heartfelt sanctification and somehow allow religious legalism to take over. In Second Timothy 3:5, the Lord instructs us to avoid those who have a form of godliness, but deny its power. Their power is only in their form. They have no real power in God. They become men-pleasers, not God-pleasers. If we strive to please and satisfy the demands of others, we have become caught in the trap of legalism.

The Secret Things Revealed

In the coming visitation, the true judgments of God will be made manifest. We must have a real commitment to personal holiness and sanctification. God wants a people who live to please Him, and our true character is best revealed in our private place. We may hide our sins from man, but we cannot hide from God. He makes the secret place His habitation. The Lord dwells there and sees us as we really are.

When speaking about the people's sin, Isaiah 3:17 says, "Therefore the Lord will strike with a scab the crown of the head of the daughters of Zion, and the Lord will uncover their secret parts." Psalm 90:8 says, "You have set our iniquities before You, our secret sins in the light of Your countenance." Whatever occurs in secret, God will manifest openly. He searches the secret things and exposes them for all to see. This is why it is important to develop intimacy with Him. Then when our innermost secrets are uncovered, it will mean blessing.

God exposed David's secret place the day he faced Goliath. How glad David must have been to have such a wonderful and real relationship revealed to the entire house of Israel. His name became synonymous with courage and power. "Is this not David the king of the land? Did they not sing of him to one another in dances, saying: 'Saul has slain his thousands, and David his ten thousands'?" (1 Sam. 21:11).

Later in David's life, God again revealed the secret place. This time, however, sin was exposed as God sent Nathan the prophet to reveal the secrets of David's heart (see 2 Sam. 12). When David committed adultery and murder, he seemed to forget that God dwells in the secret place. God's judgment brought the death of his child, the result of his sin with Bathsheba. Ecclesiastes 12:14 says, "For God will bring every work into judgment, including every secret thing, whether good or evil."

When the early Church was birthed in great power, the apostles' main objective was to reach the Jews, just as Jesus had done. God, however, had another plan. The Scriptures tell of a man named Cornelius, a centurion of the Italian regiment, whose prayers and alms went up before God as a memorial (see Acts 10:4). God took notice of Cornelius when no one else did. The disciples would never have approached this man with the gospel; so God intervened for him. God gave a vision to Cornelius and to the apostle Peter to get them into the stream of blessing that God was pouring out. Cornelius was rewarded openly by being the firstfruits of the Gentile church. Cornelius' secret walk opened the door for the Spirit to move on his behalf and the same power opened the wisdom of Heaven to Peter in a vision so he could go to Cornelius. Profound power is loosed because of our secret-place walk with God.

In the past few years, we have seen many secret things in the Church brought to light that have been an embarrassment to the Body of Christ. Yet what we've seen has just scratched the surface. Many churches are filled with people who are hiding their true selves. They may look very holy on the outside, but on the inside they are corrupt, full of dead men's bones.

He who dwells in our hearts knows our thoughts, feelings, and personal desires. Although we may have personal and intimate experiences with God, we must continually build upon those experiences. Intimacy with God is a way of life. It is not enough to have had an intimate experience with God in the secret place. We need to have a purity of relationship that the Father can reveal as a light to the world.

God's Desire for Purity

Today, morals are predicated upon our humanistic society where human ideals and interests dominate over truth. Instead of dealing with the true issue of sin, society's answer for AIDS is to promote condom usage. Their answer to babies conceived in fornication is birth control and abortion. People believe that since they are not hurting others, what they do is their own business. As long as the mess can be cleaned up or the consequences taken care of, they continue to justify their actions.

If our society does not consider God's principles, we will fall to devastation like Sodom and Gomorrah. The widespread practice of the wickedness of these cities far exceeded homosexuality. The root sins of Sodom were pride, fullness of bread or self-sufficiency, abundance in idleness, and disregard for the poor. They were a haughty people who were only concerned about satisfying themselves.

Like Sodom and Gomorrah, our society today has turned sex, or intimacy, into an open and very public issue. The world no longer distinguishes between public and private life. This is a serious mistake and the repercussions are devastating.

As Christians, we need to have the mind of God—and His main concern is people. The work of God is always people-oriented. God gave man power over His creation, crowning him with glory and power (see Ps. 8:5-6). Jesus gave His life so we could have life. However, the way to life is not through our thinking, but through the power of His Word. Romans 12:2 says, "And do not be conformed to this world, but be transformed by the renewing of your mind, that you may prove what is that good and acceptable and perfect will of God." Then you will be able to present your body as a living sacrifice, holy and acceptable to God, which is your reasonable service (see Rom. 12:1).

God wants us to present ourselves to Him as undefiled. Overeating, smoking, drinking, using drugs, etc., are harmful to the body, yet none of these things cuts us off from God. The only sin that defiles our temple is sexual sin (see 1 Cor. 6:18). It is impossible to have a physical relationship with someone without it becoming spiritual. The two become one flesh, according to the Word (see 1 Cor. 6:16).

If we do not sanctify the innermost part of our beings, our secret place, we violate our relationship with God. The purity of our secret place is a true indication of our spiritual condition and relationship with Him. God deals with spirit, and those who worship Him must worship in spirit and in truth (see Jn. 4:24).

One may wonder what the Church can offer our young people as ground for standing against sexual sin and its acceptance in our day. The Church in America is very similar to the Corinthian church. We live in the midst of people given to all manner of sexual uncleanness. The spiritually-perceptive person is vexed in his spirit as righteous Lot was in the city of Sodom (see 2 Pet. 2:7-8). Surveys indicate that the standard of holiness is not rising against this onslaught of sin; young and old alike are overwhelmed by temptation. The problem will only be resolved when our minds are renewed to see things as God sees them.

Commitment, Not Covetousness

In Revelation 14:1-5, John saw the Lamb of God standing on Mount Zion. With Him were 144,000 having His Father's name written on their foreheads. These marked ones sang, as it were, a new song before the throne of God. No one could learn this song except the 144,000 marked ones who were redeemed from the earth. These people were the ones not defiled with women, for they were virgins. They followed the Lamb wherever He went.

These were not simply virgins in the physical sense. These represent the virgins that Jesus spoke about who were called to prepare themselves for the coming of the Lord. They are not angels, but they are the ones who have been redeemed from among men as firstfruits to God.

Firstfruits speak of offering the best to God. These virgins are those who are totally surrendered to God. God knows who they are and He marks them for blessing. Be assured that God is aware of your needs and circumstances and, above all, your commitment to Him. These virgins have the highest possible commitment to God. Whenever the Scriptures speak about intimacy or sexuality, it refers to the private aspect of a relationship. Committing our sexuality to God is indicative of our attitude toward God. Sexual sin is closely related to idolatry; the two always seem to go hand in hand, for they emphasize the secret desires of the heart.

We have seen sexual sin exposed in church leaders over the past few years. Be assured that it is only symptomatic of a much deeper problem. The root problem is covetousness, which manifests itself through sexual uncleanness, despising of authority or government, presumption, pride, and self-will (see 2 Pet. 2:10). These symptoms may be made manifest in many different ways, but the root is always covetousness. In Luke 12:15, Jesus said, "Take heed and beware of covetousness..."

When man first disobeyed God in the garden of Eden, the reason was covetousness. Man coveted the place that belonged to God and despised God's right to exercise His will over them. Man tried to usurp God's authority and government, choosing his own will over the Father's, presuming that he could make it on his own. The result was sin; Adam and Eve knew they were naked. This was not just intellectual under-standing. They were intelligent enough to know that from the beginning. When they sinned, they lost their robe of righteousness and became conscious of their sinful condition. They were no longer God-conscious; they were now self-conscious. The emphasis of fallen man is always on self and it will manifest in covetous practices. This state can only be changed by getting to the root of the problem, which is the condition of the heart. The Father wants our hearts focused on Him.

God wants to bring to light the private lives of His undefiled children (those who have pure hearts for Him) for glory and honor. If we lack God's authority in our lives, it is because we do not have private holiness. A virgin keeps herself only for her betrothed. Unex-posed sin is rampant in the Church today, but the Father is marking those who are willing to commit even their private lives to Him.

This is a time when the Lord desires to sanctify us. We must separate ourselves from things that even hint of sin. Anything that leads our hearts away from God must be cut off. He asks us to commit ourselves to Him in areas that only we know we have committed to Him. He will prove our faithfulness and obedience. The Lord wants to see if we will go wherever He leads us.

The Concerns of the Committed

Revelation 14:5 says of the 144,000, "And in their mouth was found no deceit, for they are without fault...." These have no facade and do not practice deception in any way. They know that what God sees is what really matters. They do not have one standard in their public lives and another in their private lives. Their commitment and devotion to the Father and His purpose is all that concerns them. Their private consecration to God then gives birth to the song of the Lord.

A person with this heart not only desires personal sanctification, but also carries the burden for the perverseness of the land. Ezekiel was told by God to go through the holy city and place a mark on the people who sigh and cry over the abominations that are done in the holy city (see Ezek. 9:4). Those who have the mark of the Father on their foreheads are those who have a burden for the city.

The call of the Father is our corporate concern for the whole city. This is the reason the marked ones are on the mountain with the Lamb. They know the importance of communion and intercession with Him. God has a special place in His purpose for those who have a heart for His city. In Obadiah, verse 21, the Scriptures say, "Then saviors shall come to Mount Zion to judge the mountains of Esau, and the kingdom shall be the Lord's."

The Calling of a Davidic Heart

This company of marked ones is being appointed now. This is not a calling for the distant future but for today. Although the Book of Revelation is written with much symbolic language, the 144,000 need not be a literal number. Twelve (the number of divine government) is the number of God's foundation for the city. The 12 apostles of the Lamb are set aside by God for this specific purpose. The number 144 is a multiplication of the Church's foundation, just as the 24 elders (the number of a priest) contain the number 12 as a denominator. The thousands come from the multitudes; all of them come from the 12. This great company of people will be redeemed for His purpose.

In these last days God will proclaim His Word from His holy mountain. It is time for the redeemed to gather on the mountain of God. We must prepare ourselves to receive His mark by accepting the burden that He has for the earth.

People who have a personal relationship with the Father are concerned about His house. The Father notices how each individual affects the whole; He is concerned with how His house is being built in our day. David, the man after God's own heart, was the only person in the Scriptures who carried the dream for the Father's house. In the Psalms, we read how important it was to him. He declared that he would rather be a doorkeeper in the house of God than to dwell in the tents of the wicked (see Ps. 84:10).

David built the house of Israel into a strong nation and established Zion to be the site of the temple or dwelling place of God. Jerusalem was chosen to be the holy city or the capitol of the Kingdom. Through his inspiration, these places became synonymous with all that God would do in the earth.

As you read the Psalms and the prophetic books, there is a continuity of expression regarding the fulfillment of God's plan by the Church described as Jerusalem, Mount Zion, or the holy nation. Isaiah said, "Now it shall come to pass in the latter days that the mountain of the Lord's house shall be established on the top of the mountains, and shall be exalted above the hills; and all nations shall flow to it" (Is. 2:2).

How extraordinary to think that the Lord visited a young shepherd boy tending his father's sheep because he had a willing heart. David desired that God would come and commune with him. God placed a dream in David's spirit for the holy nation of Israel and exalted him to a position where he could accomplish great things. David's secret or private place was a habitation for God that was eventually seen by everyone throughout the land and recorded for many future generations.

Before the Lord first came into my life, I remembered feeling lonely. I'm not sure why I felt that way. I was from a very large family, but I was a private person and felt intimidated by the world. My sensitivity only seemed to make life more difficult. However, I did have a vivid imagination and often I would just live in my own little world. I had big dreams, but my small world did not have enough room for them. God knew that if my dreams would ever come to pass, my world needed enlarging. This could only happen by Him coming into it.

When Jesus came, I was really too young to understand. All I know is that He became real to me. He became vital to my life. My mother had always instilled

God's values into me, but religious upbringing is not enough. I met God personally and because of my relationship with Him, I have everything I could ever want. Because I welcomed God into my secret place, I have seen the transforming power of this relationship. God has prepared my life for such a time as this.

When I dedicated this book, God confirmed this to me in a prophecy spoken by Kelley Varner, Senior Pastor of Praise Tabernacle in Richlands, North Carolina. He said, "Even from your mother's womb, I've reached for you. And from a tomb, which seemed to you as loneliness, but to Me was sweet communion, I have beckoned and you have answered. And now we walk in union...." The secret emptiness in my life became a dwelling place for God. God desires to dwell in us and to manifest His glory through us.

When God comes to us and we allow Him to dwell in that innermost part of our beings, He promises to pour out of that secret place a river that will never run dry, a life-giving stream for us and everyone we meet. First Corinthians 2:9 declares, "...Eye has not seen, nor ear heard, nor have entered into the heart of man the things which God has prepared for those who love Him." God has revealed them to us by the Spirit. In this place, we enter into a union with God, receive His mind, and know His heart. We then become an active part in the plan of God for the earth.

In this book I have shared my experiences and the many wonderful things God has worked in my own life. Indeed the fruit of the righteous is a tree of life (see

Prov. 11:30). The farmer must be first a partaker of the fruit (see 2 Tim. 2:6). After having tasted the fruit of this walk, I can say, as David did, "I have tasted of the Lord and He is good; blessed is the man who trusts in Him" (see Ps. 34:8). God is faithful. God wants to use you today as a vessel to reveal His glory to the world. He wants you to partake in the blessing that will proceed from the Father's house.

My earnest prayer is that you will see at least a glimpse of the great blessing that awaits you. "Ho! Everyone who thirsts, come to the waters; and you who have no money, come, buy and eat. Yes, come, buy wine and milk without money and without price" (Is. 55:1). "Incline your ear, and come to Me. Hear, and your soul shall live; and I will make an everlasting covenant with you—the sure mercies of David" (Is. 55:3). As you set yourself on a journey to know God, you will be brought into the glory of the holy God of Israel—the same glory that will be revealed in the Father's house.

If you would like to learn of other related material available to you, please write or call:

Mt. Zion Temple
4900 Maybee Road
Clarkson, MI 48348

(810) 391-6166